"And Then Chi Chi Told Fuzzy..."

"And Then Chi Chi Told Fuzzy..."

More than 250 of the Greatest True Golf Stories Ever Told

DON WADE
Foreword by Ken Venturi

CONTEMPORARY BOOKS
A TRIBUNE COMPANY

Library of Congress Cataloging-in-Publication Data

Wade, Don.
    "And then Chi Chi told Fuzzy . . ." : more than 250 of
the greatest true golf stories ever told / Don Wade;
foreword by Ken Venturi.
       p.   cm.
    Includes index.
    ISBN 0-8092-3545-5 (cloth)
    ISBN 0-8092-3210-3 (paper)
     1. Golf—Anecdotes.   I. Title.
GV967.W25   1995
796.352'0207—dc20   94-47957
                                                 CIP

Illustrations by Paul Szep

Published by Contemporary Books, Inc.
Two Prudential Plaza, Chicago, Illinois 60601-6790
Manufactured in the United States of America
International Standard Book Number: 0-8092-3545-5 (cloth)
                                         0-8092-3210-3 (paper)

10   9   8   7   6   5   4   3   2

CONTENTS

FOREWORD

From the time I took up the game as a boy in San Francisco, golf has been a central part of my life. And while I love the competition and everything that goes with it, many of my favorite times have been those spent with friends, both on and off the course, trading stories about the people and events that are so much a part of golf history.

I remember touring California with my mentor, Byron Nelson. I'll always be grateful for the way he shaped my game, but I'll never forget all the wonderful stories he told me about players he had known over the years. When I turned pro I got to meet many of these people, and they proved to be every bit as remarkable as Byron's stories had made them out to be.

When I joined the Tour in 1957, it was a very different place than it is today. Players would spend a lot more time together. In fact, more often than not you'd drive from tournament to tournament with your friends. As you can imagine, a lot of stories were told—and retold—during these trips, and often the stories got better each time around.

That's why I'm so pleased to write the Foreword for this book. One of the things that makes golf unique are the people who are a part of the game—both pros and amateurs—and this book captures their spirit. Many of the stories are funny. Some are sad. Some are about people who showed tremendous grace and courage, both in good times and bad, in victory and defeat. All of them help give the reader a real feel for the game. If you have a friend who can't comprehend why people are so taken by golf, do them a favor: let them read this book. Then they'll understand.

I've known Don Wade since the early 1980s. In that time we've worked together on a variety of books and videos. We've played a lot of golf together and spent a lot of time just talking about the game. He's a good listener, and this book—just like its predecessors, *"And Then Jack Said to Arnie . . ."* and *"And Then Arnie Told Chi Chi . . ."*—proves it.

I hope you enjoy it.

—Ken Venturi

PREFACE

E very now and then, when I look at writers who have to cover other sports or the Real World, I'm struck by how glad I am that I get to deal with golfers. That's especially true when I'm working on a book like this, in which the stories point out the courage, grace, humor, and very real foibles of golfers. To paraphrase F. Scott Fitzgerald's observation on the rich, these golfers are just like the rest of us, only more so.

In the seventeen or so years I've been with *Golf Digest*, I've often been asked who is my favorite golfer. Of course, there is no one favorite, but if I were going to build a composite, that person would have these traits:

Dave Marr's and Amy Alcott's sense of humor; Peter Thomson's mind (and not just about golf); Tommy Bolt's ability to hit shots; Bill Campbell's devotion to amateurism; Ben Crenshaw's respect for the game's history; Jimmy Demaret's enjoyment of people; Sam Snead's and JoAnne Carner's sheer love of competition; Walter Hagen's self-confidence; Seve Ballesteros's charisma; Ben Hogan's single-minded pursuit of perfection; Tom Kite's work ethic; Harvey Penick, Davis Love, Jr., and Bob Toski's devotion to teaching; Doc Middlecoff's ability to tell a story; Nancy Lopez's grace under pressure; Arnold

Palmer and Lee Trevino's love affair with the game; Curtis Strange's intensity; Tom Watson's integrity; Tom Weiskopf's honesty; Byron Nelson's character; Ken Venturi's courage; Jack Nicklaus's record.

And Bob Jones's aura of greatness.

ACKNOWLEDGMENTS

There's always a risk when a writer sits down to acknowledge and thank the people who have been helpful in a book like this. If you don't watch yourself you wind up sounding like the idiots at the Academy Awards ceremonies. By the time they finish, they've recited their Christmas card list and people are passing out in the aisles. I'll try to keep this brief.

First, I'd like to thank all the players, writers and television guys who keep coming through with stories for these books. I appreciate the help, but I appreciate their friendship even more. I'd like to particularly thank the people at *Golf Digest*, especially Jerry Tarde and Nick Seitz, for their support and encouragement.

I'm convinced that one reason these books have done so well are the illustrations by Paul Szep, who is a genius at all this and has two Pulitzer Prizes to prove it. It helps that he loves the game. It helps even more that he's a true stand-up guy and one of the best pals you could ever have.

Ken Venturi was both kind and generous enough to write the Foreword, just as he's always been in all the time I've known him. People who never had a chance to see him play have no idea how good he really was . . . and still is. People who count him as a friend are blessed.

I'm convinced that my agent, Chris Tomasino, keeps me as a client for one reason only: it's a way to get her name in a golf book and impress all her friends in New York whose impression of the game comes from the Ralph Lauren ads in *GQ*. My life would have been immeasurably easier if I had known Chris earlier. Of course, she'd probably have a nervous tic by now.

Nancy Crossman, my editor at Contemporary, really deserves most of the credit for these books. She took a chance on the first one and has lovingly supported and promoted the next two. She is patient and understanding about the two areas that concern writers most—deadlines and advances—by forgiving the former and speeding along the latter. In a world that has more than its share of whack jobs, she's as solid as they come.

And finally, my thanks to Julia and the kids—Ben, Darcy, and Andy—for all their love, support, and humor. They've given up more than their fair share of evenings and weekends so I could get this done on time. You guys are the best. Thanks.

Earlier this year Julia decided to take up the game, probably in self-defense. When I called my friend Mary Lou Bohn at Titleist-Foot Joy to tell her the news, there was a pause.

"I would have thought being married to you would be punishment enough," she said.

Probably.

Anyway, this one's for all of you.

"And Then Chi Chi Told Fuzzy..."

ARCHITECTS

Pete Dye popularized the use of railroad ties and similar thick boards on American golf courses beginning in the 1960s, but they've been used in the British Isles since the 1800s.

When architect C. B. MacDonald was building a course in the early 1900s, he used ties to reinforce the steep face of one of his bunkers. It worked fine until one of the members tried to play out and his ball caromed off the wood, striking him on the head and knocking him unconscious.

The ties came out a few days later.

When architect Hugh Wilson was designing the elegant East course at Merion, he wanted to ensure that the bunkering would play an aesthetic, as well as strategic, role. So, as he laid out each hole he had workers spread white bedsheets where the bunkers were planned.

The result was the famous "White Faces of Merion," which are so much a part of the course's charm and challenge.

The bunkering at Oakmont, while every bit as famous as that at Merion, was not nearly as scientifically planned. The club's founder, Henry Fownes, set out to build an exacting and punishing course patterned after the classic Scottish links. The greens would be hard and fast and heavily contoured.

But it is the bunkering that sets Oakmont apart. Fownes's belief was that an errant shot should be a shot lost. Greens and landing areas were guarded by huge numbers of bunkers; at one time there were over three hundred.

How did Fownes decide where to place the bunkers? Whenever he was playing with friends and someone hit a poor drive or approach, Fownes would order a bunker placed where the shot had landed. Over the years, the number of bunkers has been reduced, but the ones that remain are still extremely difficult to play from.

Another aspect of Oakmont's early bunkers were the deep furrows created by the heavy rakes used to groom the coarse, dark river sand that were a unique feature of the course.

"If Rommel had to deal with furrows like these he'd have never gotten out of Casablanca," Jimmy Demaret once observed.

In 1935, the United States Golf Association insisted that the bunkers at Oakmont not be furrowed. Oakmont said, in so many words, take your Open somewhere else. The USGA gave in. In 1953, the two sides at least managed a compromise. The fairway bunkers would remain furrowed. The greenside bunkers would be left alone.

Of course, the furrowed bunkers didn't bother everyone. On the eve of the 1953 U.S. Open, Ben Hogan was asked about the controversial bunkers.

"I don't care if they furrow them or not," he said. "I don't plan to be in them."

Clearly, he wasn't in many of them. He went on to win

with a 5-under-par score of 283—good enough to beat his great rival Sam Snead by six shots.

When the club switched to a softer, lighter sand, they stopped furrowing the bunkers entirely, to the relief of many participants in the numerous national championships that Oakmont has hosted—and to the chagrin of the members who take an almost masochistic pleasure in their course's infamous difficulty.

"I never understood what the controversy was about," said one member. "The bunkers weren't any more penal than a water hazard."

A. W. Tillinghast, who designed courses such as Winged Foot, Baltusrol, and the San Francisco Golf Club, was a celebrated figure in the post-World War I era. In the years leading up to the Depression, he earned millions of dollars in fees. But a series of poor investments led to his financial downfall, and he spent the last years of his life running an antique shop in Los Angeles.

When Herbert Kohler decided to build the two courses at Blackwolf Run just north of Milwaukee, he decided that architect Pete Dye was just the man for the job.

In Dye, he would be getting a skilled and imaginative man. He would also be getting someone as strong-willed as he was—and who also had very definite ideas about course architecture.

Although Kohler and Dye generally got along very well—and the courses turned out to be magnificent—the two men did have their moments. . . .

On one occasion, they were involved in a discussion over the shape and placement of a hole. As they stood at the site of the hole surrounded by construction equipment, John Green, one of Kohler's employees, noticed that a tire on Kohler's car had gone flat. Now, Kohler's car wasn't a Jeep or an Explorer or a Land Rover or any other make suited to off-road work. No, Kohler would drive his Jaguar across the muddy, rocky terrain.

"I interrupted Mr. Kohler and Pete to mention the flat tire," said Green. "I know they heard me, but they barely paused in their discussion. The next thing I knew, they got in his car and drove off. Actually, as they drove away I noticed he had two flat tires."

But it was during the design of the par-3 17th hole at the River course that the two men had their most celebrated difference of opinion. After looking at the setting for the hole, Kohler decided he wanted the green tucked to the left, near the river. Not only did he think the river would give the hole an added aesthetic appeal, but placing the green here would also preserve a stand of trees he particularly admired.

For his part, Dye wanted the green set more to the right, shortening the walk to the 18th tee. The two went back and forth, unable to reach a reasonable compromise.

Several days later, Dye announced that he had to have a decision. He waited. And waited. And waited.

Finally, at about five in the afternoon, he went out to the site of the hole armed with a power saw. He waited a little longer, then simply cut down the trees and left town. Kohler was not pleased, to say the least. Still, it's a terrific golf hole.

D r. Alister Mackenzie is best known for his designs of Cypress Point and Augusta National, but he also designed a wonderful course in Michigan named Crystal Downs. His partner in this project was Perry Maxwell, who was a distinguished architect in his own right.

At one point in their collaboration, Maxwell left the site for a while, expecting Mackenzie to complete a routing plan in his absence. When he returned, Mackenzie proudly showed him his design.

"Well, tell me what you think," Mackenzie said.

Maxwell diplomatically pointed out that while it was a splendid effort, it had only seventeen holes.

L arry Wien wasn't a golf course architect, but as you'll see, he came close to becoming one in his pursuit of realizing what is surely every golfer's dream.

Wien was a successful and wealthy real estate developer in the New York City area. How successful? Let's just say he was involved in developing the Empire State Building and leave the rest to the imagination.

One day Wien was playing at his home course, Birchwood Country Club in Westport, Connecticut. The course was particularly crowded that day, and when Wien came off the course he was complaining about the languid pace of play. Finally, one of his friends had a suggestion.

"Larry, you've got enough money," he said. "Why don't you build your own golf course?"

Wien decided to do just that. He got in his car and began driving around the back roads in lower Fairfield County. It didn't take long for him to find a beautiful, rolling piece of property not far from his home. He didn't know whether the land would be good for a golf course, but he knew the price was right. And so the deal was done.

Today, if you're driving through Easton, Connecticut, and see the Connecticut Golf Club, tip your cap to the memory of Larry Wien, who found the perfect solution to slow play: build your own course.

TOMMY ARMOUR

Tommy Armour came to the last hole of the 1927 U.S. Open at Oakmont leading the championship. In those days, crowd control wasn't what it is today and the gallery often got close enough to talk with, and sometimes distract, the players.

After hitting a good drive, Armour approached his ball, selected his club, and prepared to play his shot.

"You're supposed to be such a great player, Armour," said a man in the gallery. "Let's see you get this one close."

Armour hit his 3-iron approach ten feet from the hole.

"Will that do?" he asked the man.

"Yes, but just barely," said the man.

☙

Tommy Armour was a machine gunner in the British army during World War I. During one engagement, he suffered a shrapnel wound that cost him his sight in one eye.

One day, playing a tournament in the States, he drew a young man for a caddie who was nervous about working

for such a great player. At one point during the match it began to rain, and the caddie pulled Armour's umbrella from his bag. As he did, he hit Armour in the face with the umbrella.

"Son, I only have one eye as it is, and if you poke that one out I'm going to have a hard time finding my wallet," Armour said.

AUGUSTA
NATIONAL GOLF CLUB

Jack Stephens, who succeeded Hord Hardin as chairman of the Augusta National Golf Club in 1992, is one of the wealthiest men in America. His fortune is measured in the billions of dollars, and yet he has never forgotten his modest upbringing in Arkansas.

One day Stephens set out to play at Augusta with a foursome that included a guest, who had just met Stephens for the first time. When they got to the first tee and agreed to a match, the guest was astonished that Stephens insisted on playing a $2 nassau.

"Two dollars!" the man said. "Why, I never play for less than a $100 nassau."

He remarked on it more than once during the match, and when they returned to the clubhouse to play gin, he was even more incredulous upon learning that Stephens played for a penny a point.

"Usually we play for a dollar a point at my club," the man said.

"How much are you worth?" Stephens asked the man in his slow Southern drawl.

"About $12 million," said the man.

"Let's cut the cards for it," said Stephens, absolutely serious about the bet.

The game proceeded smoothly from there . . . at a penny a point.

O

One of Jack Stephens's predecessors as chairman of Augusta National was the autocratic Clifford Roberts, who along with Bobby Jones, founded the club in the early 1930s.

One of Roberts's closest friends, and a prominent member of Augusta National, was President Dwight D. Eisenhower. Ike, a passionate if not terribly skilled player, was particularly vexed by a large tree that blocked the left side of the 17th fairway, not far from the tee. The President drove into it so often that it became known as "Ike's Tree." He wanted it cut down. Roberts wouldn't hear of it.

One year, at a meeting of the club's membership, Roberts gave a brief report on the state of the club and then asked if there were any questions.

"Cliff, about that tree on 17," Ike began.

"If that's the only question, I move we adjourn," said Roberts, interrupting Ike and ending the meeting. At Augusta, after all, there are presidents and then there was Clifford Roberts.

O

In 1959, in the midst of Arnold Palmer's remarkable string of wins in the Masters, a quiet unassuming player named Art Wall won the Masters by making birdies on five of the last six holes. Wall had already won eight tournaments in his career, but he was best known for his uncanny record on par 3s.

On the evening before the final round that year, Wall attended a cocktail party and was approached by a local resident.

"Ain't you Art Wall?" the man asked.

"Yes," said Wall shyly.

"Ain't you the guy what's made all those holes-in-one?"

"Yes sir, thirty-four of them," said Wall.

"Who you tryin' to kid," said the man. "Bobby [Jones] ain't made but three."

Originally, the Masters was called "The Augusta National Invitation Tournament," and Bob Jones resisted all suggestions that the name be changed to the Masters. In 1939 he gave in, although he often said the Masters was "a name rather born of immodesty."

Most golf fans know the story of Gene Sarazen's dramatic double eagle on the 15th hole in the final round of the 1935 Masters. The 232-yard approach shot set up a playoff with Craig Wood the next day, which Sarazen won.

Sarazen always said that as far as he was concerned, the most impressive thing about the shot was that it was witnessed by Walter Hagen, his playing companion, and Bob Jones, who had walked down from the clubhouse to follow his friends in.

But there was one other great player who was there at the time and saw the shot.

"I was playing the 17th hole and had hit my drive down the right side of the fairway," said Byron Nelson, who was twenty-three at the time. "Gene's drive was on the right side of the 15th, so I had to wait until he played and the gallery settled down before I could hit my second shot."

Incidentally, club officials were so sure that Craig Wood was going to win that the check with his name on it had already been written.

And while today the players regard the 15th as a hole that you almost always go for in two, that was far from the case in earlier days. When the Sarazen Bridge was dedicated in 1955, forty-five players hit shots from the same spot Sarazen played his historic 4-wood. Only one—Sam Snead—hit an iron, and only ten reached the green. Freddie Haas's shot came the closest to the hole— four feet, one inch.

And to neatly tie up this story, it was Freddie Haas who, as an amateur, ended Byron Nelson's remarkable string of eleven straight wins in 1945 by winning the Memphis Invitational.

Even as late as 1958, the Masters remained a somewhat casual affair, at least compared to the way it is played today.

That year Dr. Cary Middlecoff was leaving his hotel to drive to the course, when he was approached by a man carrying a golf bag.

"He was very friendly and asked if I could give him a ride to the course," Doc recalls. "I thought he must have been an amateur that I'd met and just didn't recognize. We drove to the course and walked into the locker room. He changed his shoes and was out on the putting green when people began to get suspicious. They finally figured out that he wasn't a player and threw him out. They were nice about it, though. They let him buy a ticket and come back in."

In 1957 Doug Ford was attending the National Golf Show, and he signed up for a contest to pick the Masters champion and the winning score. Naturally, Ford picked himself and put down a winning score of 283.

Less than a month later, Doug Ford won the Masters with a score of 283. He also won a $50 savings bond for making such an accurate pick.

In the early 1950s Don Cherry was not only a fine
golfer—good enough to play in the Masters—but also
a popular nightclub singer.

During one Masters he was booked to sing in an Augusta nightclub, along with a comedy act and a woman
dancer. He was headlined as "The Singing Master."

Masters officials, which is to say Clifford Roberts and
Bob Jones, were none too happy about this. On day two
of his act, he was billed simply as "A Singing Master."

The Masters is an invitational event, which means that,
while there are certain requirements for qualification,
the bottom line is that club officials have the first and
final say over who gets into the field.

In 1947 Frank Stranahan, who would go on to win the
British Amateur in 1948 and 1950, broke one of the
club's practice-round regulations and was warned that
any further problems could result in his invitation's being
revoked.

Stranahan, who was, to say the least, a strong-willed
individual, was on his best behavior the following year.
Apparently, his best wasn't good enough. Early in a
practice round he got into an argument with the head
greens keeper, and before he could even make the turn
he was approached by a group of club officials and informed that his invitation had been yanked.

Stranahan asked for a chance to explain.

The committee wasn't interested.

15

Stranahan wrote a letter of explanation and apology. No luck.

Nothing was left for Stranahan to do but to buy a ticket and watch from the gallery.

In 1987 Bernhard Langer, who had won the tournament two years earlier, was playing a practice round in front of then-chairman Hord Hardin and some other members. Langer, who can be maddeningly deliberate, particularly in practice rounds, was holding Hardin's group up—a particularly egregious mistake in view of the fact that Hardin loathes slow play.

Finally, Hardin's group played through. Afterward, their displeasure was made known to Langer—along with the not-so-subtle reminder that the Masters is "an invitational event—and that applies to Masters champions as well."

Clifford Roberts had a reputation as a dour, stern autocrat who believed in the old maxim that there are only two ways to do things: "My way or no way."

In truth, Roberts was remarkably open to suggestions about how Augusta National and the Masters might be improved. And while it's certainly true that he wore neither his sense of humor nor compassion on his sleeve, there is evidence that he occasionally was capable of exhibiting both virtues.

On one occasion, in answer to a question from a writer, Roberts began by noting, "As Jesus said, and I agree . . ." and then went on and offered up a story from the Bible to make his point.

At the time, writers didn't think it was odd that Roberts would invoke Jesus' name, although some were surprised that the answer wasn't "As I've said, and Jesus agrees . . . "

Nevertheless, at the club's annual Members Jamboree that year, a brief film was made that made light of Roberts's biblical reference and put his standing at the club in perspective.

The film showed Roberts hitting a shot from the 16th tee, followed by the ball going into the hole for an ace. Roberts and his caddie then walked toward the pond fronting the green, where a narrow deck had been placed just under the waterline.

With Handel's "Messiah" playing in the background, Roberts walked out onto the submerged deck; in the film he appeared to be walking on water. A few steps out, he motioned for his skeptical caddie to follow. Naturally, the caddie began dropping deeper and deeper into the water as Roberts looked on from above. Just as it appeared that the caddie was about to go under, a graphic reading, "Oh, Ye of Little Faith" came on the screen.

It brought the house down, and no one laughed longer or harder than Clifford Roberts.

One year British writer and television commentator Henry Longhurst fell ill and was taken to a local hospital. While in the hospital, he told some of his fellow writers that he was worried he would be unable to pay for his treatment.

Like everything else at Augusta, word of Longhurst's plight got back to Roberts, who quietly called in one of Longhurst's friends.

"Please tell Henry not to worry about his hospital expenses," Roberts said. "They will all be taken care of."

Pat Summerall had a wealth of sports and broadcasting experience by the time he came to Augusta to work his first Masters for CBS Sports. Unfortunately, not much of it was in golf, so he was pretty nervous when he went to meet with Clifford Roberts for the first time.

Roberts asked him what his handicap was.

"About an 8," said Summerall, somewhat perplexed by the question.

"That's fine," said Roberts. "The best announcer we ever had was Chris Schenkel, and he was an 18, so you'll be all right."

In 1994, Pat Summerall did his twenty-seventh and final telecast of the Masters for CBS Sports. In appreciation, Augusta National gave him a lifetime clubhouse badge, only the second the club has ever awarded. The first went to Chris Schenkel, another veteran announcer. In addition, the club made Summerall a member of the "Television Committee," which oversees CBS's coverage of the tournament.

"I guess this means I'll be Frank's boss now," joked Summerall, referring to his longtime producer and director, Frank Chirkinian.

In the 1978 Masters, Japan's Tommy Nakajima was playing well until disaster struck on the par-5 13th hole. By the time he was finished with the hole, he had used up thirteen shots and had managed to shoot himself out of the tournament. Later, in an interview, he was asked if he had lost his composure.

"No lose composure," he said, ruefully shaking his head. "Lose count."

In the early years of the Masters—until the mid-1950s—Calcutta betting pools were a big part of the tournament. People would bet thousands of dollars on the outcome of the tournament, with the favorites selling for the highest amounts.

In 1948, few people gave Claude Harmon much of a chance. The field that year included the likes of Sam Snead and Ben Hogan. Harmon sold for $450, and when he won, the man who had him in the pool took home over $10,000.

SEVE BALLESTEROS

Few have ever played with Seve Ballesteros's intensity and passion. That, plus his considerable genius, was at the heart of his tremendous popularity.

One day a writer asked Seve if he felt he should "give something back to the game."

"I have given my life to golf," Seve replied. "I have nothing left to give."

One day Seve joined a friend for a round of golf. Naturally, they had a little something riding on it, and when the match was over, Seve had lost over $100. Thinking quickly, he decided to write a check, figuring that his friend would save it as a memento of their match rather than cashing it. He figured wrong.

"Thank you, Seve," the man said. "I think I will store this along with my other valuables—at the bank."

THE BAUER SISTERS

Alice and Marlene Bauer, daughters of a teaching professional from Eureka, South Dakota, were charter members of the LPGA. They joined the Tour in 1950, when Marlene was only sixteen and her sister was twenty-two. Their talent, along with their youth and striking good looks, made them immediate drawing cards on the fledgling tour.

A few eyebrows, however, were raised when Marlene married her sister's ex-husband shortly after their divorce. The sisters' marital ups and downs, although painful for them, at least kept the struggling tour on the sports pages of the country's newspapers.

Not long after her divorce Alice remarried but this marriage wasn't destined for a long run either.

"We were incompatible," she says. "We both loved spectator sports. The problem was, he was a spectator and I was a sport."

DEANE BEMAN

Before becoming the commissioner of the PGA Tour, Deane Beman had a fine playing career, particularly as an amateur. He won two U.S. Amateurs and a British Amateur, and was a member of four Walker Cup and four World Amateur Cup teams. He joined the Tour at the age of twenty-nine, and although his six-year playing career was hindered by injuries, he did win four times before becoming commissioner in 1974.

Unlike many successful amateurs, Deane Beman did not come from a wealthy family. As a result, he often had to scramble to come up with the money to play in the top amateur events.

As a member of the 1959 Walker Cup team, he knew his expenses for the trip to Great Britain would be paid by the USGA. But Beman wanted to stay on that side of the Atlantic to play in the British Amateur, and to do that he'd have to come up with more money than was in his bank account at the moment.

If Beman lacked money, one thing he never lacked was confidence—in either himself or his golf game. To raise money for his extended stay, he went out and jacked up the stakes on whatever matches he could find. After only one weekend, he had enough money to pay for his trip to the British Amateur. A few weeks later he was the British

Amateur champion, having beaten fellow American Bill Hyndman, 3 and 2, in the final.

⛳

Deane Beman was never a long hitter, but what he lacked in power he more than made up for with a devastating short game. A case in point was the 1958 Anderson Memorial tournament at Winged Foot Golf Club just outside New York City.

He and his partner arrived at the club too late to get a hotel room, so they slept on benches in the locker room.

In the final round, he watched as one of his opponents, Bob Sweeny, holed a bunker shot on the 8th hole. Calmly, Beman ran in a long for the halve.

"The key in match play is to always expect the worst," he recalled. "No matter how tough a shot your opponent faces, assume he'll make it. That way you won't be shocked if he does."

Later in the final round of the Anderson, Beman shocked a few people himself. The finals ended in a tie, forcing a playoff. Beman faced an incredibly difficult putt on the first hole of the playoff. He was ninety feet from the hole, and the putt would break at least ten feet. He made it, surprising everybody except himself.

⛳

Deane Beman's first trip to the Masters was not as a player but as a member of the gallery. And a nonpaying member at that.

Traveling north from a tournament in Florida with a group of teammates from the University of Maryland, Deane and his companions decided to stop in Augusta. Since it was the middle of the night, they parked by the course's 4th hole and scrambled over a fence.

The following year, 1959, Beman was invited to play in the Masters. He arrived at the club, and was met by Bob Jones and Clifford Roberts. When Jones welcomed him to his first Masters, Beman confessed that it was really his second. Then he explained the circumstances under which he'd been there the year before.

Jones erupted in laughter.

PATTY BERG

By any standard, Patty Berg was one of the game's finest players and greatest ambassadors. She was one of the founders of the LPGA and won fifty-five professional tournaments over her career. Just as important, though, was her dedication to the game's growth.

Throughout her career, Berg traveled around the world staging clinics for Wilson Sporting Goods. By her own estimation, she has given over ten thousand clinics and exhibitions, inspiring countless numbers of people to take up a game that has suffered from its image as a diversion for only the wealthy elite. Her clinics were notable for her superb shotmaking, easily understood instruction, humor, and boundless enthusiasm.

Still, it's important to note how great a player she was. At the height of her playing career, much of the press attention was focused on Babe Zaharias. But in terms of sheer talent, there was no comparison between the two. The Babe could overpower a course with her raw athleticism. But Patty Berg was an artist . . . a genius, even.

Patty Berg grew up in Minneapolis, in a devout Roman Catholic family of comfortable means. The third of four children, she was a red-haired, freckle-faced tomboy who loved beating the neighborhood boys at whatever sport they were playing. She had a particular fondness for football.

"I was the only girl and the only one who could remember the plays, so they let me be quarterback of the 50th Street Tigers," she says. "Bud Wilkinson [the future Oklahoma football coach] was the captain. I'd come home scraped and bruised, and all my clothes would be ripped to shreds. That's when my mother laid down the law. I needed to find another sport. Fortunately, my father loved golf, so golf became my love. And it's been that way ever since."

That Patty Berg would become one of the game's greatest champions wasn't immediately apparent. Her first tournament was the 1933 Minneapolis City Championship. She qualified—barely—for the last flight with a score of 122. In the first round she struggled terribly and was beaten easily.

After congratulating her opponent, she began the long walk back to the clubhouse. On the way, she decided to spend the next year working exclusively on improving her game. She would take lessons and practice fiercely; she was determined to play in the championship flight the following year.

Patty was the medalist in the qualifying round of the

1934 Minneapolis City Championship and went on to win the tournament. And she never looked back. She would soon dominate amateur golf, and she later became one of the best players on the tour she helped to found.

In the early 1990s, Patty Berg was the guest speaker at a Women's Golf Summit. After a rousing speech that earned her a standing ovation, she was asked what she would change if she could live her life over.

"Not a thing," she said. "I couldn't possibly be this happy or lucky again."

TOMMY BOLT

Tommy Bolt was a majestic shotmaker, but his putting often left something to be desired. Consequently, it didn't take much to try his patience when he was on the green.

In one tournament he was standing over a putt when somebody in the gallery moved, casting a shadow over the ball.

"Lord," he asked, looking toward the heavens. "How do you expect a man to make a putt in the dark?"

Tommy Bolt always took a lot of pride in his sense of style. In fact, the easiest way to get a rise out of him was to tell him how much you admired Doug Sanders's kaleidoscopic sartorial sense.

One evening Tommy arrived for a Legends of Golf dinner in a magnificently tailored, white silk, double-breasted jacket, dark slacks, and a matching tie and handkerchief.

"Tommy," a friend told him, "I just want your old clothes."

"Can't have them, son," said Tommy. "I give my cast-offs to Doug Sanders."

♧

While Tommy genuinely liked writers and enjoyed seeing his name in print as much as the next guy, on some occasions he was more approachable than on others.

Coming off the course after a bad round at the U.S. Open one year, he was met by writers who wanted an interview.

"Don't you newspaper sons of bitches have something to do out on the golf course?" he fumed.

♧

During one tournament, Tommy Bolt was being heckled by a person in the gallery. After a while, Tommy lost his patience and told the man off, using some fairly colorful language to help make his point. A few holes later he was approached by a tournament official, who fined him $50. Tommy handed the official a $100 bill and told him to keep the change.

"When I see that guy he's gonna hear it from me again, so you might as well take your money now," he said, walking off.

♧

Tommy Bolt's greatest win came in the 1958 U.S. Open at Southern Hills. He had been playing very well coming into the tournament, and as the Open went on he seemed to gain confidence. It wasn't until later that he revealed he had been carrying a card on which was written this message: "God, grant me the serenity to accept the things I cannot change, the courage to change the things I can, and the wisdom to know the difference."

Whenever he got a bad bounce or hit a poor shot—and there weren't many that week—he would quietly pull out the card and ponder its message.

Jimmy Breslin, the celebrated New York City-based newspaper columnist, got his start as a sportswriter by covering the 1958 U.S. Open—probably one of the few times he ever set foot on a golf course.

He followed Tommy Bolt in the last round of the Open, and after Bolt hit his drive on the final hole, Breslin approached him with a suggestion:

"You're going to win anyway," he said. "Go ahead and throw a club."

JULIUS BOROS

Julius Boros, who won two U.S. Opens and a PGA Championship, was perhaps best known for his casual, almost carefree approach to the game. Unlike players today, many of whom turn pro even before they finish college, Boros didn't join the Tour until he was thirty. One winter day, while working as an accountant in Connecticut, he looked out the window during a blinding snowstorm and asked himself what he was doing there when he could be playing the Tour down in Florida.

Boros made up for his late start by winning eighteen tournaments on tour, the last being the 1968 Westchester Classic, when he was forty-eight. A writer once asked him when he was planning to retire.

"Retire to what?" he replied. "All I do now is play golf and fish."

There were always a lot of kids running around the Boros household, because there were six Boros children and their friends were always welcome.

One morning Julius Boros decided to sleep in. As he dozed, one of the neighborhood kids wandered into the bedroom looking for a drink of water. Boros woke up and, seeing the child in the darkness and naturally assuming it was one of his, reached out and pulled the kid onto the bed. Then he fell off to sleep again, leaving the youngster to lie there wondering what in the world was going on.

Julius Boros won the 1952 U.S. Open and was a favorite to repeat a year later at Oakmont Country Club. There was just one problem: Boros forgot to send in his entry form and had to spend the week of the Open fishing.

The next year, however, he won the Open in a playoff with Arnold Palmer and Jackie Cupit at The Country Club in Brookline, Massachusetts. At the awards presentation, he proved that he had a long memory.

"I want to thank the USGA for letting me play this year," he said.

Of all of Julius Boros's children, Guy Boros has been the most successful at following in his father's footsteps. He was playing in the 1994 Colonial Invitational, with a good chance of winning, when he learned that his father had died. He thought about withdrawing but decided to finish the tournament, reasoning that it's what his father would have wanted. He wound up finishing 12 shots behind the winner, Nick Price.

WALTER BURKEMO

Walter Burkemo was a marvelous player who won the 1953 PGA Championship and lost in the finals twice. One year, during the PGA, he was approached by a fan who asked a perplexing question.

"Mr. Burkemo," the fan said politely, "I was just wondering how come when you address the ball you sometimes take four waggles and other times you take five?"

Burkemo bogied the next three holes as he tried to figure out the answer himself.

BURNING TREE CLUB

The Burning Tree Club in the Washington suburb of Bethesda, Maryland, has long been known as "The Club of Presidents" because of its tradition of giving an honorary membership to sitting presidents. President Jimmy Carter ended this practice when he declined the membership in a repudiation of Burning Tree's men-only admissions policy.

Without getting into a debate over the pros and cons of men-only clubs, suffice it to say that Burning Tree has had to spend considerable effort in recent years defending itself against critics—political and otherwise—who believe their policy is an insulting anachronism. Others argue that the club is just taking the right of free association to its logical conclusion. Either way, the debate—and Burning Tree—are not about to go away anytime soon.

The policy has led to some interesting occurrences over the years, such as the time a member offered to put up the money to build a swimming pool. Now, a swimming pool would be a splendid addition to any club or home in the Washington area, in view of the severity of the area's summer weather.

But when the offer reached the Board, it was refused.

The logic went something like this: If we had a pool, members would want to bring their kids. If the kids were small, they'd need some kind of supervision. Supervision usually means lifeguards or baby-sitters. Either way, they are often female.

No, thank you, to the pool.

A nother time a small plane crash-landed on one of the club's fairways. Fortunately, no one was injured. Unfortunately, one of the passengers was a woman. She was quickly shown the gate.

T hen there was the time that a detail from the Secret Service came to the course to secure it for a presidential visit. One of the agents was a woman. She was the agent who made sure the area near the front entrance was safe and sound—because that's as close as she got to the property.

A ll this makes it sound as though the men-only rules are hard and fast, but there is an exception. Women are allowed in the clubhouse on one day during the Christmas season—to do their holiday shopping in the pro shop.

CADDIES

Peter Thomson, the elegant Australian who won five British Opens in the 1950s and 1960s, arrived for the Open one year and was approached by Cecil Timms, who had caddied for Ben Hogan when he won the 1953 British Open at Carnoustie.

"Laddie, I'm the best and I'm choosing you," he said to Thomson. Thomson, who never relied on a caddie to do much more than carry the bag and stay out of the way, hired Timms, but was decidedly unimpressed . . . as was Ed Furgol, who had won the U.S. Open in 1954. He had heard about Timm's skills and asked him to caddie for him in the British Open. It was a short-lived team. Furgol became so infuriated with Timm's attitude that he threatened to beat him with a sand wedge.

An American journeyed to Scotland on holiday, looking forward to experiencing all the pleasures of playing golf in the game's birthplace. One of the things he had heard much about were the Scottish caddies, who are well known for their eccentricities and their knowledge of the game.

Naturally, he was somewhat disappointed when he arrived at one course and was told that the only available caddie was a recent immigrant who didn't speak much English.

However, off they went, and for several holes the golfer and the caddie barely spoke. The caddie was polite and worked hard, but his inability to offer advice began to frustrate the golfer. Finally, after hitting a pretty good shot, the golfer turned to the caddie and asked what he thought. The caddie thought long and hard, trying desperately to come up with just the right words. Finally it all came together.

"Bloody fluke, sir," he said, beaming.

T he Jigger Inn, next to the 17th hole at the Old Course at St. Andrews, is a favorite gathering spot for local caddies and tourists alike. One evening during the 1990 British Open, one of the former was regaling a group of the latter with stories about the Americans for whom he had caddied over the years. One story concerned a Yank whose interpretation of the rules was pretty liberal.

"He hit his drive off into the rough on the Road Hole over there," the caddie said. "We'd had a fair bit of rain and the rough was a little thicker than usual, so the ball was sitting down. He got to the ball before me and was pacing all about, testing the lie. I slowed down a bit to give him time, and when I finally reached the ball he asked me whether I thought it was a 4- or a 5-iron.

" 'Sir,' I said, 'you'd best hit the 5-iron. You're at least three stomps away from a 4-iron.' "

An American traveled to St. Andrews on holiday for a little golf. Although he enjoyed the Old Course, he was mystified by some of the bounces and breaks he witnessed around the greens. And although his caddie tried to help, there were times when he was as baffling as the greens themselves.

On the Road Hole, his approach missed the green, leaving a delicate and dangerous pitch. If it was misplayed there was a good chance the ball would run off the green and into the Hell Bunker. The man studied his shot from every angle, then asked his caddie what he thought the ball would do once it reached the hole.

"Well, sir, there's one thing for certain," the caddie said, peering over the golfer's shoulder as they both read the line. "When it slows down, it's really going to speed up."

Willie Turnesa, the former U.S. and British Amateur champion, was playing in the finals of the 1938 U.S. Amateur at Oakmont. After taking a comfortable lead through the first 18 holes, he dropped two holes early in the afternoon round. And when he hit his drive into the deep, punishing rough on the 12th hole, things began to look grim. After studying his lie, Turnesa reached into his bag for a club. As he did, he noticed that his caddie, a youngster barely into his teens, had tears streaming down his face. Turnesa asked him what was wrong.

"I hope we don't lose, Mr. Turnesa," the caddie said, sobbing.

"Don't worry, son," said Turnesa. "Somehow we'll win."

And they did.

Two American couples traveled to Scotland in September, usually the most beautiful time of the year to play the classic seaside courses. But as luck would have it, the weather was awful—cold and rainy with nothing encouraging in the forecast. Midway through yet another sopping-wet and chilly round, one of the women said to her caddie, "Isn't this weather unusual for this time of year?"

"Aye, that's the problem, ma'am," he said. "This isn't this time of year at all."

FRANK CHIRKINIAN

F rank Chirkinian, the longtime producer and director of golf coverage for CBS Sports, is universally regarded as the best at what he does. He is responsible for most of the worthwhile innovations in television's coverage of the game—one of the most difficult of all sports to cover. A man with fierce loyalty to the people who work with him, Chirkinian has a deep love of the game and a wonderful sense of humor.

I n 1961, Chirkinian decided to place microphones near the tees at Olympia Fields, the site of that year's PGA Championship. This was historic, since it marked the first time TV viewers could hear the swish of the clubhead and the crack of the ball at impact. Unfortunately, it also marked the first time an obscenity was broadcast nationally to a golf audience, courtesy of Don January after a poor tee shot.

The same year, Chirkinian and his crew found themselves trapped by the unpredictability of the game.

With Don January leading Jerry Barber by four shots with just three holes left to play, CBS ran out of its allotted time for golf and simply switched to other programming.

As Chirkinian and his announcers headed for the airport, Jerry Barber was pulling off what can only be described as a miracle. He ran in birdie putts of twenty, forty, and sixty feet to force a playoff. Chirkinian was waiting at a ticket counter when he heard the news of the playoff. He quickly scrambled to gather his announcers, getting one off a plane that was just about to pull away from the gate.

The PGA of America decided to hold the PGA Championship at the Dallas Athletic Club in 1963, and while no one doubted the quality of the course, some people—Chirkinian included—questioned the wisdom of holding a tournament in Dallas in July.

"Earlier in the year I asked Don January about it, and he said there was nothing to worry about," says Chirkinian. "He said that it doesn't really get that hot in July, and since he was from Texas, I figured he knew what he was talking about.

"Well, it was unbelievably hot that week," Chirkinian remembers. "At one point early in the week, I was in the locker room and they brought January in. He had passed out on the course from heatstroke."

In fact, it was so hot that when the enormous Wannamaker trophy was brought out for the awards ceremony, officials had to wrap it in towels so the new champion, Jack Nicklaus, didn't burn his hands.

BOBBY CLAMPETT

Bobby Clampett was one of the country's best amateurs when he came to Inverness for the 1979 U.S. Open. A junior at Brigham Young University, he was at the height of a collegiate career that would see him named All-American three times.

The year before, he had been the low amateur at the Open, so when the USGA needed a marker (a noncompeting player) to fill out the field in the third round, Clampett was selected.

Since his score wasn't going to count for anything, Clampett decided to add a little color to the championship. After he was announced on the first tee, he acknowledged the gallery, teed up his ball, then dropped to his knees and split the fairway—much to the delight of the spectators.

Sadly for him, the USGA was not nearly as amused. A few minutes later, another marker arrived and Clampett was asked to leave the course.

The 1979 U.S. Open, which Hale Irwin won for the second of his three Open titles, was also notable for the planting of what came to be known as "The Hinkle Tree."

While playing his practice rounds Lon Hinkle, one of the Tour's better players and longer hitters, noticed that he could hit his drive on the 528-yard, par-5 8th hole over a line of trees and into the 17th fairway, leaving himself a considerably shorter and easier approach shot. In the first round, Hinkle pulled off the shot with a 1-iron and made a birdie, and word soon spread through the rest of the field. That he also led after the first round helped draw attention to his antics.

Clearly, the USGA wasn't going to let this continue. For one thing, it gave the Open the appearance of an Elks Club outing. For another, it held up play.

So, the next day when players arrived there was a newly planted, twenty-five-foot black spruce blocking the shortcut—the first time in anyone's memory that a course had been altered in mid-championship. For his part, Hinkle wound up making two birdies, a par, and a bogey on the hole, finishing 20 shots behind the winner, Hale Irwin.

HENRY COTTON

Henry Cotton, the three-time British Open champion and easily the finest English player of his generation, was revered by his country's golfers.

Unfortunately, by virtue of his prominence, he had the dubious distinction of being named the captain of the Great Britain/Ireland Ryder Cup teams in 1949 and 1953—a time when America dominated the competition.

In 1953, with the matches being played at Wentworth, Cotton's team led well into the competition, and indeed looked as if they might win, until some sloppy play cost them vital points in the foursomes play, traditionally the Americans' weakest format.

Cotton, angry and frustrated by the performance of some of his players, said he would "kick the team's asses." Unfortunately, his comment made it into all the papers the following day. Cotton's wife, the formidable Toots, had to race out in the early-morning darkness and buy up every paper she could get her hands on, hoping to prevent a mutiny.

Cotton's team rallied on the final day, but it wasn't quite enough. The Americans held on to win by a point.

THE COUNTRY CLUB

The Country Club, in the Boston suburb of Brookline, is a bastion of classic Yankee propriety and reserve, as a new member once discovered.

As he approached his ball on the first tee, near the clubhouse, he was greeted by an indignant member, who chastised him.

"See here, good man, move back behind the markers," he huffed. "These are the rules of golf, and if you can't play by them I'll see that the Board hears about it."

"Look, I've been a member here for six months, and you're the first member who has even spoken to me," the man replied. "And by the way, this is my second shot."

JOHN DALY

John Daly was playing a practice round in the 1994 Federal Express St. Jude's Open in Memphis when he was approached by a girl selling used golf balls for a dollar apiece. Daly agreed to buy three, and paid for them on the spot. When the girl got home, she was stunned—Daly had given her three $100 bills. She told her parents, and they decided that it was an oversight and that she should go back to the course, find Daly, and return the money.

When the girl found Daly, she told him he'd made a mistake and tried to return the money, but he wouldn't hear of it.

"It wasn't a mistake," he said. "Keep it."

And for good measure he gave her an autographed ball.

BERNARD DARWIN

Bernard Darwin was a gifted writer, longtime golf columnist for *The Times* of London, and a player accomplished enough to play on the 1922 British Walker Cup team.

Like many players in the days before Gene Sarazen's invention of the sand wedge, Darwin had a terrible time when he found himself in a bunker. It didn't help matters that he was given to fierce fits of temper on the course.

One day, after a particularly nasty stretch in the sand, Darwin let fly with a string of expletives that included the Lord's name in a variety of combinations. He closed his tirade by looking heavenward and shouting, "And don't send your son down. This is a man's work."

JIMMY DEMARET

"Jimmy Demaret is the most underrated golfer in history. He played shots I'd never even dreamed of. Eventually, I learned them, of course, but it was Jimmy who showed them to me for the first time."

Ben Hogan

🏌

"I first came out on tour in 1950, and Jimmy kind of took me under his wing," remembers 1960 PGA Champion Jay Hebert. "We'd drive from tournament to tournament in that big old Cadillac of his, and that was quite an education in itself. Jimmy knew everyone and had seen almost everything over the years, and he was very generous about sharing that knowledge.

"I remember going into the clubhouse in one of the first tournaments I played in that year," Hebert continues. "We went into the bar and Jimmy told me to order a '7 & 7.' I told him I'd never heard of it.

" 'Just order it, Jay, you don't have to drink the stuff,'

Demaret said. 'Seagram [distillers] pays me $25,000 a year to represent them on tour.'

"In all the years I've been around the game of golf, it was the most perfect endorsement deal I've ever seen."

♉

"The thing about Jimmy is that he honestly liked people," remembered Dave Marr. "In the 1957 U.S. Open at Inverness, Jimmy was in the clubhouse leading the tournament. The only guys with a chance to beat him were Doc Middlecoff and Dick Mayer. Dick made a tough twelve-footer on the last hole to win by a shot. Jimmy looked at me—and I'll never forget this—he said, 'Well, I'm glad he won it. He needs the money, you know.'

"Jimmy was absolutely sincere, too. That's just the way he was."

♉

Demaret was a fixture at the old Bing Crosby National Pro-Am, which he won in 1952. One of the reasons he loved the tournament so much was that it gave him a chance to hang around with celebrities, many of whom were his friends.

"One year Jimmy was with Phil Harris at the bar and Harris was telling us about this new kid, Dean Martin," remembers Dave Marr. "Phil was in awe of how much he could drink.

" 'Hell, Phil, you could drink him under the table with one lip tied behind your back,' Jimmy said.

"Another time he told Phil that his face had enough wrinkles to hold a three-day rain," adds Marr.

Jimmy Demaret was chatting with friends outside the clubhouse at Augusta National during the 1964 Masters. He noticed three jets fly over the course.

"There go Jack, Arnie, and Gary," he joked.

A few minutes later a series of small, propeller-driven planes flew over.

"And there go their caddies," he said.

When Jimmy Demaret died in 1983 at the age of seventy-three, many of his friends traveled to Houston for the services. His widow mentioned to one of them that she was a little concerned because she didn't know if Jimmy had left her any money.

"Are you kidding? Jimmy had money in every bank in Houston," the friend replied.

Later, someone asked why he spread his money all over town.

"He had to," the man said, laughing. "He was friends with every bank president in Houston. He didn't want to hurt anyone's feelings."

HELEN DETTWEILER

Helen Dettweiler, born in 1914, was one of the driving forces behind women's professional golf in America. Although not as well known as players like Patty Berg or Babe Zaharias, she was a fine player who went on to become a widely respected teacher.

She was raised in a prominent Catholic family in the Washington, D.C., area. Although her father encouraged her golf, he was more than a little skeptical about her chances. Clearly, though, she wasn't. On the eve of the Washington District Championship, she vowed that if she didn't win she would enter the convent. By any definition, this is what's known as playing under pressure. Anyway, she won, and the Church's loss was golf's gain.

Helen Dettweiler loved to fly, at a time when women pilots were a virtually unheard-of species. And she was good enough at it that when World War II broke out she volunteered for the Women's Air Force Service Pilots and flew almost 1,000 hours ferrying B-17 bombers.

After the war, she moved to California and established herself as a top teacher in the Palm Springs area. When Katharine Hepburn and Spencer Tracy were filming *Pat and Mike* at Riviera Country Club, she was hired as a special adviser. But her greatest notoriety came from giving lessons to President Eisenhower. While vacationing in Palm Springs, he would come by every morning at 8:30. When the time came to return east, he asked how much he owed for the lessons. Helen said she couldn't possibly accept payment; rather, she considered teaching him a great honor.

Two weeks later she received from the President a painting, a landscape of his Gettysburg farm. She treasured the gift until her death in 1990.

BRUCE DEVLIN

Bruce Devlin was another in a long line of fine Australian golfers; he won eight times on the PGA Tour and several times around the world. Later, he was a popular golf analyst for NBC Sports for many years.

Devlin was a good junior player, but his game really developed when his father lost an arm in a tragic accident.

"After his accident, he grew very withdrawn and would only play golf with me," Devlin recalled. "He took a great deal of pleasure in my playing well. It helped him overcome his depression. As a result, I had an even stronger desire to excel and win than the other fellows did. I was playing for both of us."

LEO DIEGEL

There may never have been a golfer as superstitious as Leo Diegel. Of course, if you had spent most of your career being psyched out by masters of the art like Walter Hagen, you'd be superstitious too.

Once, Diegel was playing in the Los Angeles Open at Riviera. The year before, he had opened the tournament by hitting a drive out of bounds and into some stables. For some reason, this shot bothered him greatly and he thought about it obsessively. When he returned to Riviera, he was determined not to make the same mistake.

Naturally, he teed up on the first hole during the practice round and knocked the ball into the same stables. He was a wreck for the rest of the round and had trouble sleeping that night. Tossing and turning in bed, he suddenly came upon the solution to his problem.

The next morning he stood at the first tee, deliberately hit his drive into the stables, and took his penalty. Then he crushed the next ball into the heart of the fairway.

WALTER HAGEN

L ike a few other top players, most notably Byron Nelson, Walter Hagen was ambidextrous. In fact, he
could pitch well enough with either hand that the Phila-
delphia Phillies once offered him a major league contract.
During the 1929 British Open at Muirfield, Hagen's ball
came to rest against a stone wall. He simply turned the
club on its toe, gripped it left-handed, and played the
shot perfectly toward the green—to the delight and as-
tonishment of the gallery.

H agen had scant regard for deadlines, starting times,
or meetings of any sort. In the 1933 Ryder Cup
competition, played at Southport and Ainsdale, this cav-
alier attitude almost cost the American team the matches
by forfeit.

As captain, Hagen was scheduled to meet with J. H.
Taylor, the captain of the Great Britain/Ireland team, to
exchange pairings. The time for the first meeting came
and went without either Hagen or an explanation. Hagen

was a no-show for the second meeting as well. Taylor, incensed by what he took to be gamesmanship on Hagen's part, issued an ultimatum: if Hagen didn't appear for the next meeting, Taylor would pull his team out of the matches. Hagen calmly arrived on schedule, but without bothering to offer an apology.

⛳

In 1928, the height of Prohibition, Walter Hagen traveled to Royal St. George's for the British Open. While there, he was introduced to a brand of scotch that he particularly enjoyed. Knowing it would be difficult to obtain this brand in the States, he tried to figure out how to bring some home with him. After winning the championship he quickly discovered the solution to his problem.

He put a bottle in the trophy case and breezed past the customs officials in New York.

⛳

"I was paired with Walter one year in the old Inverness Four-Ball, and even though he was in his fifties then and well past his prime, I was still excited about playing with him because he had been my idol as a boy," remembers Byron Nelson. "We finished the front nine, and as we headed for the 10th tee Hagen turned for the clubhouse.

" 'Play hard, Byron,' he said. 'I'll see you on 14.'

"I'd like to say it didn't matter and that I played good enough for both of us, but the truth is we finished dead last," said Byron.

🏌

The late Charlie Price was an elegant and knowledgeable writer who grew close to Walter Hagen in the process of collaborating on a book. He was the source for many of the stories in this series of books, particularly stories about "The Haig."

"One year Hagen arrived in New York by steamship after winning the British Open," Charlie recalled. "He had given his winner's check to his caddie and was dead broke. His son, Walter Jr., wasn't much better off, but he had at least won some money betting on the deck races on the trip over. Walter borrowed enough money for cab fare to Delmonico's Hotel, where he told the front desk that instead of his usual suite, he'd take an entire floor. He then asked the desk to advance him $500 in crisp, new bills—which was the only kind of cash he'd carry.

"When they were settled in upstairs, young Walter asked his father just how he planned to pay for all this. Hagen simply summoned the hotel manager to his room, explained the situation and how much publicity the hotel would get from having the British Open champion as a guest, and then told him to come back when he'd come up with a solution—one which wasn't going to cost Hagen any money."

🏌

Hagen was a generous, if distant, father. Once he bought his son an expensive Austin roadster for his birthday. It was the perfect gift . . . for another birthday. Junior was only fourteen at the time.

♉

"Walter Hagen really enjoyed being around other people, much the same way Arnold Palmer does," remembered Charlie Price. "After winning the PGA Championship at Olympia Fields in 1925, he had gone to several celebrations, then returned to Olympia Fields, where he was staying in a cottage. When he couldn't get the door unlocked, he simply broke in, which surprised the hell out of the elderly woman who was staying there. But she was delighted to meet Hagen, offered him a drink, and sat and listened as he recounted his win for several hours."

♉

On one occasion, Hagen's casual disregard for starting times nearly caused an international incident.

He was paired with Japan's Torchy Toda in the first round of the 1936 Masters. Toda's appearance in the Masters was a matter of considerable pride among the Japanese people, and no less a figure than Hiroshi Saito, the Japanese ambassador to Washington, had traveled to Augusta for the tournament.

When Hagen and Toda's starting time came and passed, there was murmuring in the gallery. A Masters official apologized to Toda and the ambassador, explaining that this was typical of Hagen and that they should think nothing of it. Still, the Japanese were not amused.

Finally, Hagen emerged from the clubhouse, where he had been holding court with some friends. He strolled onto the tee, shook hands and apologized all around, and off he and Toda went, arm and arm, down the first fairway.

As a boy, Byron Nelson had idolized Hagen and always dreamed of the day when they might be paired together. That happened soon after Nelson turned pro, when he played his way into the lead in a tournament called the General Brock Open.

Nelson had had a sleepless night thinking about playing with Hagen, and he wasn't any less nervous as their starting time approached. He arrived on the tee and waited. And waited. And waited some more. Tournament officials asked him if he'd like to go out with another player as a marker, but Nelson declined. Finally, forty-five minutes later, Hagen arrived on the tee. He didn't apologize, but did say that he'd heard Nelson was playing very well. For his part, Nelson said he was just thrilled to be there.

Nelson went out and shot 42-35-77. Despite his disappointing performance, he very much enjoyed his first round with The Haig.

Hagen led after every round of the 1914 U.S. Open at Midlothian, finishing with a record-tying 290. As he relaxed over a drink in the locker room, a writer asked him whether it bothered him that a young, local amateur, Chick Evans, might still catch him.

"No, why the hell should it? I've already got my score."

He wound up winning by a stroke.

DAVE HILL

Dave Hill is one of the finest shotmakers to ever play the game. He was also one of the game's most outspoken players, which earned him a healthy number of fines.

His most celebrated outburst came at the 1970 U.S. Open at Hazeltine, then a new Robert Trent Jones course in Minnesota. After the first round Hill, one of the tournament leaders, was brought into the pressroom and asked what he thought about the course, which had been criticized by players all week.

"What does the course lack?" a writer queried him.

"Eighty acres of corn and a few cows," he quipped. "They ruined a good farm when they built this course."

For this insightful criticism, he was slapped with a $150 fine.

SIMON HOBDAY

South African Simon Hobday, who won the 1994 U.S.
Senior Open at Pinehurst, was unknown to American
golf fans for most of his career—a career that saw him
win six tournaments in eighteen years on the European
Tour.

Hobday is nothing if not a free spirit, as is illustrated
by the time he went to a restaurant and was told by a
rather stuffy maître d' that neckties were required. Hobday tried to reason with the man, but to no avail. If he
wanted to eat at the restaurant, he had to be wearing a
tie.

Since Hobday is by nature an accommodating man, he
left to find a tie. When he returned he was wearing the
tie—and nothing much else.

BEN HOGAN

One of the most enduring Ben Hogan stories concerns the time he was paired with Claude Harmon at the Masters. The story goes that Harmon made a hole-in-one on the treacherous 12th hole. Hogan made a birdie, and as they walked off the green, Hogan said, "Claude, you know I can't remember the last time I made a two there. What did you have?"

"Why, Ben, I had an ace," said an astonished Harmon.

"Oh," said Hogan.

Some forty years later, a salesman for Hogan's equipment company asked Hogan if it was a true story.

"I didn't remember Claude's ace then," Hogan said. "How do you expect me to remember it now?"

"People know that Ben struggled early in his career, but most people don't realize just how tough it was for Ben," remembers Harry Cooper, one of the top players in the 1930s. "His biggest problem was that he hit the ball with a low, hard hook which made it almost impossible to carry bunkers in front of greens, let alone hold the greens.

"Ben was very shy, and he'd never ask for advice, but I felt so bad for him that one day I took him aside and suggested that he hold on a little tighter with his left hand through the hitting area. This kept his hands from rolling over too quickly, and helped prevent a hook.

"Again, Ben was a very private person and he never publicly acknowledged whatever help I gave him, which was fine, but I know he appreciated it, because every time he'd see me he'd give me a big hug. That was a lot of emotion for Ben."

For a long time people—including some sportswriters who should have known better—insisted that golfers weren't really athletes. But if strength and hand-eye coordination count for anything, Ben Hogan in his prime was the very definition of an athlete.

When Hogan won the Hitchcock Belt as America's top athlete in 1953, he was introduced to former heavyweight champion Gene Tunney, who came away impressed.

"My God," Tunney said. "I shook Hogan's hand and it feels like five bands of steel."

During the years that he struggled to make it on tour, Hogan returned to Fort Worth many times with scarcely a cent to his name. In order to make ends meet, he worked dealing cards at night—one of the few jobs that would allow him to practice his game during the day.

"Ben could deal cards so they came out of his hand in a blur," remembers Paul Runyan. "His hands were remarkably quick. We used to have contests where we'd all sit around a table with a coin placed in the center. Someone would snap their fingers and we'd all try to cover the coin. Nobody could ever beat Ben. He was just too quick."

Much has been written over the years about Ben Hogan's desire for privacy, which is certainly understandable in a man who spent so much time in the public eye. But perhaps the most telling indication of this trait came when he and his wife, Valerie, had a new house built in Fort Worth.

It didn't include a guest bedroom.

In the 1980s, a producer came up with an idea for a videotape that held a lot of promise. Ben Hogan, Sam Snead, and Byron Nelson would sit down with writer Charlie Price to talk about their lives and careers. For their efforts they would each receive $50,000. Snead and Nelson readily agreed, but Hogan needed some convincing, so the producer asked Snead to give him a call.

"I said, 'Ben, I don't think you counted all the zeros in his offer,' " Sam said. " 'He's going to pay us $50,000 for one day's work. We'll all come to Fort Worth. Hell, Ben, we'll all come to your house if you want. Think it over, will you?'

"Well, Ben thought it over and decided he didn't want to do it," Sam continued. "That was just Ben's way. And there was no point in arguing with him once he made up his mind."

A few years later, a Japanese businessman approached several players of the Hogan-Snead-Nelson era with a proposition: they would all receive a generous amount of money to design one hole each for a course to be built in Asia. The agreement also called for the group to gather for a photo session—in Fort Worth, naturally.

As anyone familiar with such sessions will tell you, they are not like gathering the kids and the dog for a family portrait. Lighting has to be carefully arranged and rearranged. Light meters are read and reread. What should logically take just a few minutes can easily drag on for hours, particularly if the photographers are perfectionists facing a once-in-a-lifetime opportunity.

Clearly, this would have been the case at this photo shoot if not for Ben Hogan's own sense of timing. After about a half hour, he'd seen enough.

"I believe you fellows have all the photos you need," he said, ending the session—undoubtedly to the relief of the other golfers.

🏌️

Ben Hogan arrived on the practice tee at a tournament, and before beginning his warm-up routine, paused to study the other players working on their swings.

"Boys," he said to those nearby. "If you didn't bring it with you, you're not going to find it here now."

🏌️

Dave Marr, paired with Ben Hogan at Colonial one year, watched as Hogan made a double bogey on the first hole. As they walked to the next tee, Marr tried to console Hogan.

"Geez, Ben," he said, "tough start."

"Dave, that's why there are eighteen holes," said Hogan.

Ben Hogan was the captain of the 1967 Ryder Cup team that faced Great Britain and Ireland at Champions Golf Club in Houston. As is traditional, the captains introduced their teams at an opening dinner.

Dai Rees, the captain of the Great Britain/Ireland team, went on at length about his team's remarkable individual accomplishments, which in this era consisted largely of assorted East Sussex Four-Ball Championships and the like. These remarks were met with polite applause.

When Hogan rose to speak, he got right to the point:

"Ladies and gentlemen, it's my honor to present the United States Ryder Cup team—the greatest golfers in the world."

The fiercely partisan audience roared in approval.

They may not have been the greatest, but they were good enough to win, 23½ to 8½.

"Ben does have a wonderful sense of humor, especially once he gets to know you and becomes comfortable," explains Ken Venturi. "In 1958, I was playing very well at the Masters, while Ben barely made the cut. I was doing my interview when they brought Ben in. Suddenly the place was silent—that's how much the writers respected Ben.

" 'What is this, a wake?' Ben asked, and with that he took one of the writer's notebooks, walked up to me, and said, 'Now, Ken, tell me how you played the third hole.' "

At one U.S. Open, Hogan led by a shot going into the final round. In his postround interview a writer asked him whether he'd "rather be ahead by a shot or behind by a shot" going into the final round.

Hogan looked at the writer in disbelief.

"Would you rather be rich or poor?" Hogan asked.

"Ben knew the effect he had on other golfers and he was very good about not using their nervousness to his advantage," remembers Gardner Dickinson, a Hogan protégé. "But he was also a keen student of human nature, so sometimes he'd show up on the first tee for a practice round a little early to see how the other players would react. They'd almost always ask him if he'd like to go ahead. He'd say 'no' and then stand there by the markers watching them tee off. They were more nervous than when the actual tournament started. There'd be guys that could barely get it airborne.

"Ben also had a very good sense of humor," says Dickinson. "One day we were getting ready to tee off in a practice round and a player came up and asked if he could join us.

" 'Sorry,' Ben said, 'we already have three.' "

For all his public acclaim and the reverence in which he's held by both players and fans, Ben Hogan remains a fiercely private, even shy, man.

In 1973, he came to Augusta National to receive an award from the press. When the ceremony had ended and he had answered all the writers' questions, he left quietly. He was seen a short time later at the airport, having dinner. Alone.

Ben Hogan greatly admired both Mickey Wright's swing and her golf game. Still, that admiration had its limits. One day she asked if she could come by and watch Hogan practice.

"Yes, if you don't ask any questions," he replied.

In one of the most celebrated upsets in U.S. Open history, Jack Fleck—a virtual unknown—beat Ben Hogan in a playoff to win the 1955 Open at San Francisco's Olympic Club.

In order to get into the playoff, Fleck had to play the last four holes in 2 under par, a daunting proposition given the difficulty of the closing holes at the Olympic Club.

Gene Littler, who knew all too well how tough those holes were, put it in perspective when he was told what Fleck needed to do to force the playoff.

"Yes, he needs to birdie two holes," Littler said. "But even if he does, he still has to par the other two, and that's no bargain."

Fleck did just that.

In the 1947 Ryder Cup matches in Portland, Oregon, Henry Cotton, the captain of the Great Britain/Ireland team, caused something of a controversy when he requested that the grooves of the Americans' irons be examined. His contention was that the Americans were using illegal clubs. Hogan, as American captain, remained silent and submitted the clubs for inspection. The clubs were found to be perfectly legal, play proceeded, and the Americans won by an astonishing 11-1 margin.

While Hogan had been publicly quiet about the entire business, privately he was seething. Two years later, he made his point when the Americans traveled to Ganton, with Hogan again captaining the U.S. side.

On the eve of the matches he asked for an inspection of the British/Irish irons, maintaining that the grooves

79

were illegal. Two equipment manufacturers examined the clubs but couldn't agree on their findings. To resolve the matter, officials from both teams sought out Bernard Darwin, the respected British golf writer. Darwin, who was having dinner at the time, casually examined the evidence and made his determination.

"Nothing a little filing won't put right," he said.

Ben Hogan designed just one course in his career, the Trophy Club in Dallas. He brought to the job his legendary attention to detail. When workers couldn't get the contours of the greens exactly the way he wanted them, Hogan took over and raked them by hand.

In the 1980s, Ben Hogan was asked if he would like to compete against any of the current players.

"Just one," Hogan said. "Tom Watson."

Why Watson? Because Hogan had already beaten everyone else worth beating.

Even well into his seventies, Hogan had a remarkable ability to hit golf shots on demand. So he agreed to travel to Riviera Country Club to shoot a series of commercials for his equipment company. At the start of the shoot, he positioned himself in the center of a fairway and waited patiently for the crew to get in position. When everything was ready, the director told him to go ahead and hit the ball to the green.

"What would you like it to do when it gets there?" Hogan asked. "Bounce left, right, or back up?"

During this shoot, he also demonstrated his innate sense of fairness and his sense of humor.

Club officials had offered to close the course, or at least the holes Hogan was using, to member play. But Hogan wouldn't hear of it, protesting that it was the members' course and he was just a guest. Of course, he did take a certain pleasure in watching the members' reactions when they had to try to play through Ben Hogan.

Ben Hogan's last tournament appearance came in 1971 at the Champion's Tournament in Houston. It was a brutally hot and humid day, debilitating for everyone in the field but particularly so for a man on the verge of his fifty-ninth birthday.

Standing on the 4th tee in the first round, he faced a carry of 175 yards over a ravine on the par 3. He pulled a 3-iron, but hit three balls into the ravine before making a 9 on the hole. He shot a 44 on the front, then went double bogey, bogey on the 10th and 11th. On the 12th he hit a good drive and put his approach on the green. Then he sent his caddie ahead to the green to pick up the ball and summoned a cart to take him to the clubhouse.

"I'm sorry, fellas," he said to his playing partners. "Don't ever get old."

With that, Ben Hogan ended one of the greatest playing careers in golf history.

Ben Hogan was once asked which of his accomplishments gave him the greatest satisfaction. Was it his record in the major championships? His ability to come back from a near-fatal accident and dominate the game? His uncompromising standard of play? None of the above.

"I get the greatest satisfaction knowing that I went dead broke out on tour more than once and still came back and made it on my third try," he said.

JOE JEMSEK

Joe Jemsek, born and raised in Chicago, is one of the true heroes in American golf. You won't find his name on any list of the great champions, although he was a fine player. Jemsek's genius was his belief that the public-course golfer should have it just as good as the members of private clubs. His courses in the Chicago area—especially his beloved "Dubsdread," the No. 4 course at his Cog Hill complex—are as good as any in the region.

As a boy Jemsek caddied at Cog Hill, which was named for the original owners, the Coghill brothers. One day he was caddying for Marty Coghill himself.

"Joe, how'd you like to own this place?" Coghill asked.

"Someday I will," Jemsek answered.

In 1951, he did.

Joe Jemsek was a good player, but like Harvey Penick and others, he realized early on that his future on the Tour might be somewhat limited. This revelation came to him the first time he saw Sam Snead.

"You guys go ahead and win all the tournaments," he told Snead and Johnny Bulla one day. "I'll own all the golf courses."

At the 1934 World's Fair in Chicago, Jemsek made headlines by winning a long-drive contest with a shot that carried 501 yards into Lake Michigan. Of course, the tee was perched atop a 630-foot tower.

After that, he had people flocking to him for lessons. Naturally, like any good businessman, he raised his rates.

"I had been charging $2 for a lesson or six for $10," Jemsek remembers. "After the World's Fair, I was getting $5 a lesson."

Jemsek combined a good sense of humor with a keen eye for business. Years ago, players who hit shots into the woods found signs posted on the trees:

"If you're in here, you need a lesson from Joe Jemsek."

BOBBY JONES

After receiving his undergraduate degree from Georgia Tech, Jones enrolled in Harvard University to get a second degree in English literature. Informed that he was ineligible for the golf team because he had already lettered at Georgia Tech, he volunteered to be the team's manager. The coach reluctantly told him that the team already had a manager. Jones, eager to earn his Crimson "H," volunteered to be the assistant manager. The coach readily accepted.

One of Jones's most important duties was overseeing the team's supply of corn whiskey during road trips. As he did in almost everything he pursued, Jones handled this task with aplomb—except during a trip to New Haven for a match with Yale, for which he arrived with a buzz on, wearing a sheepish grin, and with no whiskey left for the team.

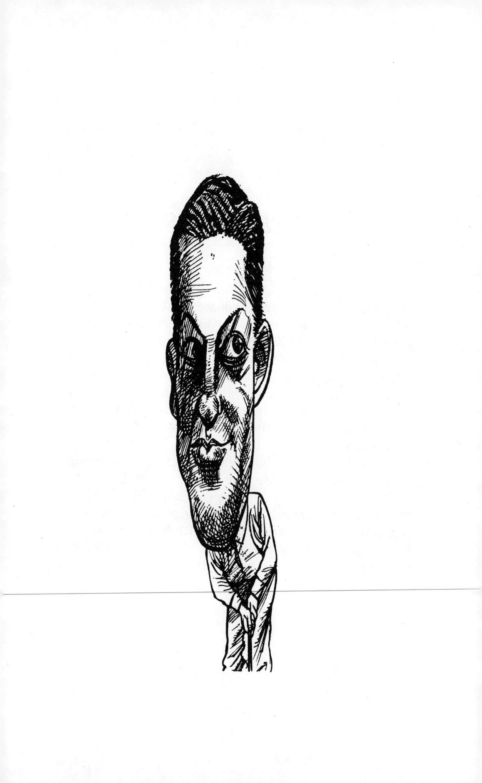

One of Jones's favorite playing companions was his father, "The Colonel," who made up in enthusiasm what he lacked in skill.

One day in the early 1940s the two paired to play Charlie Yates, the 1938 British Amateur Champion, and a local minister in a match at East Lake. The match remained close. On one of the final holes, with the Colonel getting a stroke, he put his approach into a greenside bunker. He took several swipes at the ball then compounded his misery by three-putting, after which he unleashed a torrent of obscenities.

The Jones team went on to win the match, and as the foursome was walking off the final green, the minister said to Yates, "Charlie, I should have known we'd never beat such a combination of proficiency and profanity."

Jones was stricken with syringomyelia, a degenerative nerve disease. His condition was particularly cruel because it wasted his body while leaving his mind intact. Eventually he was confined to a wheelchair, but he struggled to maintain as normal a life as possible.

One day Charlie Yates asked Jones if he was able to sign a few copies of his book.

"Yes, but not too many," said Jones, whose hands were so afflicted by the disease that he could only manage a scrawl by using a pen attached to a rubber ball. "My hands don't work so well anymore."

Yates, a dear friend of Jones, had assumed that Jones would have his secretary inscribe the books. He immediately apologized to Jones.

"Oh no, Charlie," he said. "It wouldn't be proper to have someone else sign them."

In 1926, Bobby Jones was already the best player in the world, but when he went across the Atlantic for the British Open, he had been struggling with his game. No matter how often he changed clubs, he couldn't seem to find a driver he liked.

When he came to Sunningdale, outside London, for his qualifying round, he was still searching for a club that looked good to his eye. Jack White, the professional, showed him a driver he was particularly fond of—so fond, in fact, he had named it "Jeanie Deans" after the beloved Scottish heroine.

Before he hit even one ball, Jones sensed that this was the club he'd been looking for. In the first qualifying round, he shot a 4-under-par 66 that many believe is still the closest thing to a perfect competitive round. He went around in 33-33—66, taking just 33 putts. He hit every fairway and missed just one green.

When he holed his final putt the gallery, according to a newspaper account at the time, "gave a reverential cheer and then dispersed awestruck, realizing they had seen something they had never seen before and would never see again."

After his round, Jones said, "I wish I could take this course home with me."

Indeed, so dominant and impeccable was his play that London's oddsmakers immediately made him a 3-1 favorite to win the Open at Royal Lytham—the shortest odds in British Open history. They knew what they were doing. Jones finished two shots clear of Al Watrous, to capture his first of three British Open titles. He would win ten of his thirteen major championships with "Jeanie Deans" in his hands.

In 1930, after winning the U.S. and British Opens and Amateurs and completing the Grand Slam, Jones—then twenty-eight—retired from competition.

Shortly afterward he signed a contract with Warner Bros. to produce a series of golf-instruction vignettes, which are still considered among the best ever made.

It is a measure of Jones's stature that he was paid $101,000 for his efforts while his costars—the likes of W. C. Fields, Jimmy Cagney, Edward G. Robinson, and Douglas Fairbanks—were paid nothing.

Jones completed the Grand Slam by winning the U.S. Amateur at Merion. He beat Gene Homans, 8 and 7, and as they shook hands he told him, "Gene, if you want to play again you'll have to come to East Lake for a Saturday-morning game. I'm through."

After winning the Grand Slam, almost all of Jones's tournament play was in the Masters, but it was largely ceremonial. In 1937, he came to the par-3 4th hole and hit his drive some 100 yards into the woods, where it came to rest in a stand of shrubs.

"My God," said an astonished Jones. "That's about as bad as I've ever hit a shot. The only thing worse would have been a whiff."

PRESIDENT JOHN F. KENNEDY

President John F. Kennedy loved golf and was an accomplished player—far more so than he let on to the press and public, for fear he'd be compared to former President Eisenhower, whose passion for the game was well documented and sometimes criticized. In fact, when Kennedy moved into the Oval Office, one of his first discoveries—much to his amusement—were spike marks heading from the office to a putting green on the South Lawn.

In any event, Kennedy was determined to improve, and he hit upon a novel idea that made him sort of a forerunner of today's pros.

He arranged for his personal photographer, Cecil Naughten, to take home movies of the presidential swing. After each shot, Kennedy would signal whether the ball flew straight, left, or right. He planned to send them to Arnold Palmer—to whom he often likened his own style of play—to have Palmer critique them and offer advice.

Sadly, the tragedy of November 22 occurred before the films were sent.

TOM KITE

A man came to the pro shop at the Austin (Texas) Country Club and introduced himself to the professional, Tinsley Penick, son of the much-revered teacher Harvey Penick.

"Tinsley," he said. "I'm forty-four years old and have all the money I'll ever need. I used to be a pretty good player, and I'd like to get back to working on my game. I'm thinking about the Senior Tour, and I figure if I dedicate the next six years to golf, I'll be good enough to do pretty well out there. How do you like my chances?"

Tinsley Penick took the man into the clubhouse.

"See that fellow over there having a sandwich?" said Tinsley. "He's forty-four, has all the money he'll ever need, and he thinks about the Senior Tour every now and then. Now how do you like your chances?"

The man having a sandwich was Tom Kite.

In the final round of the 1978 Hall of Fame tournament at Pinehurst's famed #2 course, Tom Kite was dueling Tom Watson. As he stood over his putt on the 5th green, Kite suddenly stepped back and announced that his ball had moved. While no one else had seen the ball move, he called a one-stroke penalty on himself. He wound up finishing in a tie for second, one shot behind Tom Watson, who won $50,000. Kite's check was for $19,333.33.

Later, writers asked Kite about the penalty.

"It was the only thing I could do," he explained. "When you break a rule, you suffer the consequences. I have to live with finishing second for a few days. I have to live with myself for the rest of my life."

In 1979, Tom Kite received the U.S. Golf Association's highest honor, the Bob Jones Award. And calling the penalty on himself at Pinehurst was only one example in a career filled with reasons why.

Tom Kite had agreed to play in an outing the day after his 1992 U.S. Open win. Certainly, people would have understood if he begged off, but Kite never gave a thought to not playing. Still, there was one thing that needed to be done.

That same day his wife, Christy, took the U.S. Open trophy to the Austin Country Club and presented it to Tom's longtime teacher, Harvey Penick.

"Here you go, Mr. Penick," she said. "Tom said this is for you."

BOBBY LOCKE

South African Bobby Locke, who won four British Opens, was not a person who minced words or worried excessively about other people's feelings. In fact, as Australian Peter Thomson once observed, Locke seemed "to take a particular joy in irritating people."

Locke was a remarkable talent. Sam Snead called him the best putter he ever saw. And although every one of his shots seemed to be a big, sweeping hook, he was a remarkably effective shotmaker.

One day Lloyd Mangrum, who shared Locke's approach to winning friends and influencing people, offered a bit of golf advice.

"Bobby, you've got too much right hand on that club," he said.

"I save the left hand for checks," Locke replied icily.

HENRY LONGHURST

Henry Longhurst was broadcasting the British Open Championship from St. Andrews one year. At one point in the tournament, he summed up the plight of an American player who was struggling with the mysteries of the Old Course.

"And there now is the 3:25 train from Dundee," he intoned. "I can see clearly her numbers—3-3-4-4-3—and if our American friend had started that way it should have been damned less boring this afternoon."

DAVIS LOVE, JR.

" After I had played the Tour for a while I decided it was no life if I was going to raise a family, so I decided the time had come to become serious about teaching," said Davis Love, Jr. "I had always had a huge amount of respect for Harvey Penick, both as a man and a teacher, so I went to see him for some advice.

" 'Davis, have you ever played a musical instrument?' he asked me, and when I told him I hadn't he said the first thing I had to do was go out and sign up for some lessons. I didn't understand what the connection was between me wanting to learn to teach and playing an instrument, but if Mr. Penick said to do it, I wasn't going to question him. I went out and rented a clarinet and arranged to take lessons from a very nice lady who lived nearby. I set off driving to her house, and the closer I got the more nervous I became. By the time I reached her house I was actually sweating. I didn't know the first thing about playing the clarinet. I didn't know how to hold it. I didn't have a clue about reading music. And then when I actually sat down with her and realized how ignorant I was, I just about froze.

"Just about at that point, I understood what Harvey

was up to. He wanted me to understand what it was like for a beginner to come for a lesson—and like so many of Harvey's lessons, it was one I never forgot."

Even though he had been a fine player—and maybe because he was and understood the pressures of competition—Davis Love, Jr., was always very nervous when he watched his son play in tournaments.

During one tournament when Davis III was at the University of North Carolina, the young Davis stood on the tee of a par-4 hole and aimed directly at the green, some 280 yards across from a pond that guarded the corner of a dogleg. With the long, beautifully rhythmic swing that his father had patiently taught him, Davis launched a drive that rose steadily up over the water and came down to rest safely on the other side. When the round was over, the elder Davis approached his son and asked him what he had been thinking about when he played the shot.

"I had 265 to carry the water, Dad," he said. "I could have missed it and still hit it that far."

At that moment Davis Love realized he had taught his son a game with which, as Bobby Jones had said about a young Jack Nicklaus, he wasn't familiar.

Davis Love III was a member of the 1985 Walker Cup team that played the team from Great Britain/Ireland at Pine Valley. Davis Jr. was watching his son's matches alongside Bob Carney, then an editor at *Golf Digest*. After young Davis hit a particularly remarkable shot, Bob turned to Davis Jr. and said, "I dream about hitting shots like that."

"Don't even dream about it," Davis replied with a smile.

LOVERS AND
OTHER STRANGERS

One evening there was a large dinner-dance at an exclusive club in North Carolina. In the course of the evening a great deal of liquor was consumed and a man and a woman, who were not married to each other, became bored with the activity on the dance floor and decided to take a walk. One thing led to another and they wound up in a greenside bunker, but not in what one might call an unplayable lie.

Suddenly, a guard showed up with an enormous flashlight and asked a simple question: "Are you members?"

"Yes," they replied as they scrambled to rearrange their clothes and retreat to the clubhouse.

"No you're not," the guard shouted, chasing after them. "No member of this club would leave without raking the bunker."

One fine day Donald Trump, the New York real estate developer and darling of the tabloids, decided that his then girlfriend, Marla Maples, should learn to play golf. So off they went to Winged Foot, where Marla changed into new golf clothes and headed toward the practice tee for a lesson from one of the assistant pros. All of this would have been uneventful if the route from the pro shop to the driving range had not taken her past the men's grill.

When she reached the practice tee, she was delighted to see that it was virtually deserted.

Not for long.

In the time it takes to finish a beer and change back into a pair of spikes, the range had become packed with men who had decided their swings needed a little work.

In the early 1960s, two friends met in the final round of the English Match Play Championship. As one of the players knelt down to study a putt, he noticed something out of the ordinary and asked his opponent to come over and have a look. Knowing it's against the rules for opponents to give advice to one another, the second player begged off.

"No, really, come take a look at this putt," he said. "It's quite extraordinary."

The second player came over and looked, but confessed he didn't see anything unusual.

"Study the complete line of the putt," he was instructed by his friend.

The player took another, longer look and then turned to his opponent.

"I say, that one in the yellow isn't wearing any knickers, is she?" he said.

Dutch Harrison was a talented player in the Snead-Nelson-Hogan era. He was colorful, to say the least, and was widely known as one of the game's greatest hustlers. On top of that he had nerves of steel, as he proved one day during a run-in with his wife—one of the three he'd have in his life.

Harrison was preparing to tee off on the first hole of a tournament when his wife approached him with a gun, threatening to shoot him.

"Well, honey, go ahead and get it over with if you're going to shoot me," he said.

His wife, astonished, simply turned and walked away. Harrison teed up and shot a 67—the low round of the day.

GEORGE LOW

"George is a wonderful man, but if you loan him money you might as well write it off as a gift," says Dave Marr with a laugh. "In the winter of 1948, George was tapped out and he talked Claude Harmon into loaning him a couple hundred dollars. The loan went unpaid for several months. In April, Claude won the Masters. As he was walking to the awards ceremony to get his green jacket, George approached him and tried to hand him the $200.

" 'Oh, that's OK, George,' Claude said. 'Forget it.'

"George always did have a great sense of timing."

"Another time I won a bet with George and the payoff was that he had to pay for a dinner for my wife and me and another couple," says Marr. "I asked Gary and Vivienne Player to join us, and we had a wonderful time. I didn't find out until later that George had borrowed $100 from Gary to pay off the bet. I'm glad Gary enjoyed the meal he bought, because I'm sure George never repaid him."

LLOYD MANGRUM

L loyd Mangrum was, by any measure, a tough guy. He was decorated for bravery in World War II after serving as an infantryman in Europe. His pencil-thin mustache and cold, dark eyes made him seem especially menacing.

One year, at a players' meeting, the Tour's policymakers announced that there would be substantial fines for players who used obscenities on the course.

"Listen to me you little ****," he said. "You **** can't **** tell me how the **** I **** want to **** talk. If you want to **** fine me, do it now."

DAVE MARR

Dave Marr, who won the 1965 PGA Championship and went on to a long and successful career as a golf analyst for ABC Sports, NBC Sports, and the British Broadcasting Corporation, is a person of uncommon wit and intelligence.

In 1986, the U.S. Open came to the exclusive Shinnecock Hills Golf Club on Long Island. The championship opened on a stormy Thursday, with the wind howling off the Atlantic. As Marr stood near the first tee watching the early players go off, a member of the gallery, who had just bought some food, dropped some dollar bills, and the wind carried the money racing along the ground.

"Welcome to Shinnecock," Dave said. "The only club in America where they overseed with pictures of dead presidents."

S tanding nearby was Hans Kramer, who handles Dave's affairs for Mark McCormack's enormous International Management Group. Kramer helped the man retrieve his money as it tossed along the ground.

"See how fast Hans moved when he saw some loose money?" Dave said. "Mark taught him that. Of course, if it had been Mark he would have kept twenty percent."

GARY McCORD

Back in the bad old days before he caught on as an announcer for CBS Sports, Gary McCord was just another guy struggling to make a living on the PGA Tour. Actually, it's not fair to label him as part of any single group. He's always been unique.

Not the least of his virtues is his willingness to press his luck. One time he was summoned to meet with Augusta National chairman Hord Hardin, who had the authority to approve McCord's participation in CBS's Masters coverage.

McCord and CBS producer/director Frank Chirkinian went to Hardin's office, where Hardin explained the belief among Augusta's officials that the telecast should be reserved and dignified—two adjectives that don't usually spring to mind in connection with Gary's appeal as a broadcaster. As the meeting wound down, Hardin asked McCord if he had any questions.

"Just one. I guess this means I'm not wearing my clown suit, huh, Hord?" McCord asked.

In the mid-1980s, *Golf Digest* sent a writer to California to do a profile on Gary McCord. The writer and McCord decided to fit in a little golf along with the interview. Since the writer didn't have any clubs, they drove to a rental warehouse where McCord was storing much of his worldly belongings—clubs, clothes, furniture, the works.

"You must not have much stuff left at home," the writer said.

"This *is* home," said McCord.

In 1976, Gary McCord decided to test the Tour's policy on facial hair. He arrived at the Houston Open with a beard and was immediately told by officials to either shave or face a fine and suspension. McCord complied by cutting the beard back to a Fu Manchu. Soon after, he sent a copy of the Tour's regulations to the American Civil Liberties Union, which assured him that if he took the Tour to court he'd win. A couple of weeks later, the Tour told him he had to shave everything off. ACLU or no ACLU, McCord knew when he was beat. Out came the razor. Off came the mustache.

JOHNNY MILLER

In 1993, after six years without a victory, Johnny Miller won the AT&T National Pro-Am at Pebble Beach. It was a remarkable win that, among other things, ensured that Miller would be invited to play in that year's Masters, where he'd had three second-place finishes.

Even though he was talented and had a remarkable record, he was almost forty-seven years old, and nobody expected him to win at Augusta. But that's not to say there wasn't any pressure on him.

"My four sons are going to caddie one round each," Miller said. "That's a lot of pressure. If I miss the cut, two of them are going to get stiffed."

Alas, he missed the cut by a shot—and two of them did get stiffed.

In 1973, Johnny Miller stunned the U.S. Golf Association—and his fellow players—by shooting a record 63 in the final round of the U.S. Open at Oakmont to win.

The next year Miller came to Winged Foot as one of the favorites to win the Open, but his chances ended in one of the course's numerous and difficult bunkers.

"The sand was heavier than I thought, and it only took me four swings to figure it out," he said.

On the Monday prior to the start of the 1973 U.S. Open, a woman approached Miller and introduced herself as a clairvoyant.

"You are going to win the Open," she said. "I am never wrong."

She did the same thing throughout the week, meeting Miller as he came off the final green after each round. Naturally Miller was more than a little skeptical. But after he opened with a round of 71 and followed it with a 69, he started to believe. When the woman didn't show up on Saturday and he shot a 76, he wasn't quite sure what to think.

Prior to his final round he received an unsigned telegram predicting victory for him. Clairvoyant or not, he shot a 63, passed twelve players, and won the championship.

MYOPIA HUNT CLUB

The Myopia Hunt Club, in the suburbs of Boston, was founded by the four sons of the mayor of Boston, Frederick Prince. Since they were all nearsighted, Myopia seemed like a particularly appropriate name.

Over the years the club's membership has included some of the area's most prominent names, including one rather eccentric Yankee whose exercise regime was unusual, to say the least.

He'd get up early in the morning, walk out to a hole near his house, and hit a bag of balls into a pond with his driver. Then he'd shed his clothes, dive into the pond, and swim around until he had retrieved all the balls.

BYRON NELSON

There's a school of thought that great players develop in pairs. Tom Kite and Ben Crenshaw, who grew up together in Austin, Texas, are an example that comes immediately to mind. But the best example is Byron Nelson and Ben Hogan, who first met as caddies at the Glen Garden Country Club near Fort Worth. When they were both fourteen, they played in the caddie championship, both shooting 40s in the nine-hole match. Byron won the playoff by a single shot.

"Byron was very influential in my career," remembers Miller Barber, who won eleven tournaments on the regular Tour and twenty-four times on the Senior Tour. "I used to caddie for him and shag his practice sessions when he was the pro in Texarkana. We'd play matches for a dime, but what I remember most is watching him practice. I've never seen anyone hit the ball so consistently straight. I think the real reason I went bald so fast is that he kept bouncing balls off my head."

B yron Nelson's first wife, Louise, who died in 1985, was a saintly woman totally devoted to her husband and his career. But in 1935, after over a year of marriage, she did have a small bone to pick with him.

"Byron, in the whole time we've been married you've bought four new drivers and I haven't had a new dress or a new pair of shoes," she said gently. "Either you don't know what kind of driver you like or you don't know how to drive."

B yron Nelson was playing in the final round of the Hershey Open when a strange thing happened to him.

"I drove it right down the middle of the fairway and the ball disappeared over the hill," Nelson recalls. "We came over the hill and couldn't find my ball. And we couldn't have confused it with one of the other players' balls because it had my name on it. Well, it was quite a mystery, but I played a second ball and the penalty meant I finished fourth instead of third, which was a $300 difference. A short while after the tournament, I received $300 in money orders in the mail. It turned out a woman had seen my ball and, not knowing the game, just put it in her purse and walked off."

Byron Nelson was playing in the 1945 Tam O'Shanter tournament in Chicago, which at the time offered the biggest purse in golf. The tournament organizer was George S. May, a promotional genius.

In one round, when Nelson made the turn in 34, May was there to meet him on the green. In front of a huge gallery, he bet Byron that he couldn't shoot another 34 on the back.

He was right. Byron shot a 32 and collected $100.

Byron Nelson wrote one of the first best-selling golf books, *Winning Golf*. It sold 130,000 copies at $2.50 each. Although Nelson enjoyed being a best-selling author, he was practical about the monetary benefits.

"I told my wife Louise, 'That little book just bought us fifty head of cattle for the ranch,' " he said.

Byron Nelson is very soft-spoken and a gentleman in the truest and best sense of the word. But anyone who believes he isn't competitive to the core is mistaken. One person who learned this the hard way was Frank Stranahan.

Stranahan was the heir to a healthy fortune who went on to win the British Amateur in 1948 and 1950 and lost in the finals of the U.S. Amateur in 1950. By most accounts, Stranahan could be difficult at times and was perfectly capable of trying the patience of a . . . well, a Byron Nelson.

Nelson was the professional at Inverness, where Stranahan's family had a membership. Stranahan's father insisted that Nelson give his son lessons, but the younger Stranahan proved intractable, insisting on doing things his way—Nelson's playing record and reputation as a teacher notwithstanding. Finally, Byron just gave up.

One day Stranahan came into Nelson's pro shop with two friends and challenged Nelson to a match. Nelson declined at first, but there was something about Stranahan's attitude that lit up Nelson's competitive fires.

"I'll tell you what, Frank," Nelson said. "Not only will I play you, but bring along your two friends, too. I'll play your best ball."

Nelson went out and shot a record 63 on a course good enough to have hosted three U.S. Opens and a PGA Championship.

JACK NICKLAUS

J ack Nicklaus was a twenty-year-old amateur when he
arrived at Cherry Hills near Denver for the 1960 U.S.
Open. He had won the National Amateur the year before,
and while few people thought an amateur could win the
Open, the supremely confident Nicklaus wasn't one of
them.

"Jack, the odds are 35 to 1 against you," his father,
Charlie, told him just prior to the start of the championship. "What do you think? Do you want to bet on yourself?"

"Darned right, $20 worth," said Jack.

"Win, place, or show?" his father asked.

"Win," said Jack.

And he almost did. Paired with Ben Hogan in the final
round, he finished second to Arnold Palmer. After the
round, writers were congratulating the forty-eight-year-
old Hogan on his ninth-place finish, a fine showing.

"Hell, I played with a kid who should have won by ten
shots," said Hogan.

J ack Nicklaus came to the 1962 U.S. Open at Oakmont
Country Club having turned pro earlier in the year.
While he had yet to win as a pro, he was already established as one of the game's best players, and the Open
was billed as a duel between the twenty-two-year-old
Nicklaus and the thirty-two-year-old Arnold Palmer, then
at the peak of his career and the Tour's most popular and
dominant player. The location of the tournament only
added to the drama. Oakmont, just outside of Pittsburgh, is near Palmer's hometown of Latrobe, and Palmer
was very much the favorite.

The two tied at the end of four rounds, and as they
prepared to tee off in the playoff, Palmer asked Nicklaus
if he wanted to split the purse, a common practice in
those days.

Nicklaus didn't give it a moment's thought.

"No, Arn," he said, "that wouldn't be fair to you.
Besides, you don't really want to do that, do you?"

He then went out and won his first professional title,
71 to 74.

M ass interviews at golf tournaments, particularly the
majors that attract a lot of writers who don't ordi-
narily cover the sport, don't exactly resemble "Meet the
Press."

One year at the Masters, a reporter asked Nicklaus,
"Jack, how did you find the course?"

"Well, I've been coming here a long time, and it's
pretty well marked by road signs," he said with a laugh.
"I really didn't have a problem."

J ack Nicklaus is meticulous about every aspect of his game. It is inconceivable that he'd be penalized for a rules violation or, even worse, for signing an incorrect scorecard.

In 1963, after Nicklaus won the Masters, Bob Jones, Clifford Roberts, and everyone else waited while he checked and signed his card.

"If he had gone to [Jones's alma mater] Georgia Tech instead of Ohio State, he'd have been able to add his score by now," joked Jones. "Maybe we should give him a two-stroke penalty for 'delay in signing a scorecard.' "

I n 1966, four of Nicklaus's friends en route to Augusta to watch Jack play in the Masters—including a friend from childhood, Bob Barton—were killed when their plane crashed. Nicklaus was devastated and considered pulling out of the tournament. But his friends and family convinced him to play, so he did. He dedicated his performance that week to his friends.

Nicklaus opened with a 68 that was even better than it sounds, in view of the difficult playing conditions. He wound up winning the tournament by beating Tommy Jacobs and Gay Brewer in a playoff.

On the Saturday night before the final round of the 1986 British Open at Turnberry, Jack Nicklaus and Tom Watson were having dinner with their wives when Greg Norman stopped by to say hello. It was a timely visit.

"Good luck tomorrow, Greg," Nicklaus said. "Just relax and don't let your grip pressure get too tight."

It was good advice. Twenty-four hours later, Norman had won his first major championship.

If there was ever any doubt about Jack Nicklaus's will-power, it should have been erased following his win in the 1962 U.S. Open at Oakmont in a playoff with Arnold Palmer. It wasn't just the win, but something that happened afterward.

Nicklaus was watching a highlight film that showed him standing over a short putt with a cigarette dangling from his lips. At that moment, he resolved never to smoke on a golf course again, because he felt it set a bad example for kids. And he hasn't since that day.

You could easily make a convincing argument that Jack Nicklaus is the greatest golfer in history. You could also make a good case that he's the worst caddie in history.

Like his father before him, Jack Nicklaus is his kids'

biggest fan. And while he realized early on that any of his children who chose to follow in his footsteps faced a daunting task, he has always been there to support them, encourage them, and share in their successes and failures.

One way he did this was by caddying for them, although it did not always work out as well as planned. One time, caddying for Jack Jr., he managed to lose a ball on the first hole. Another lapse saw Team Nicklaus, this one made up of dad and son Gary, fail to count the number of clubs in Gary's bag. By the time they realized their oversight, Gary had incurred a four-stroke penalty for carrying an extra club—a particularly odd mistake by a man who, it is said, used to read the Rules of Golf from cover to cover before the start of each season.

GREG NORMAN

During the 1994 British Open at Turnberry, there was considerable controversy over the cost of staying at the nearby Turnberry Hotel. In fact, many American players elected to skip the championship and stay home. A writer asked Norman if the hotel was breaking him financially.

"It might if I tried to buy it," he said.

OAKMONT COUNTRY CLUB

Chick Evans came to the 1919 U.S. Amateur Championship at Oakmont as the defending champion, having won the title in 1916 at Merion—the last time the championship was played prior to American involvement in World War I.

Naturally Evans, who would win the title again in 1920, was a favorite, but the hard, fast greens were too much for him to handle this year. After hitting three poor putts on the 15th hole, he handed his putter to his caddie and finished the hole using the handle of his umbrella.

Prior to the 1983 U.S. Open, the United States Golf Association told Oakmont to keep the rough playable. Naturally, the membership ignored the orders and grew the roughs to their customary thickness—and let them grow nine inches tall for good measure. After all, they reasoned, why should Oakmont play easier for the U.S. Open than it does for a member-guest?

Well, the roughs were, for all intents and purposes, unplayable. If you hit your ball into the rough, all you could do was try to pitch it back into play and hope for the best.

A lovely little standoff developed. The USGA ordered the roughs cut. Oakmont said no.

The USGA then ordered the greens superintendent, Paul Latshaw, to cut the roughs.

The membership told Latshaw that if he cut the roughs he was history at Oakmont. Not just a part of Oakmont history. He was history. Down the road. Gone.

Happily for Latshaw and the players, Oakmont relented and the roughs were cut before Saturday's round.

PORKY OLIVER

Porky Oliver, who won the 1958 Houston Open, was a happy-go-lucky guy whose abilities were often overlooked because he was such a free spirit. And, like many players of that era, he enjoyed playing the horses.

After he won at Houston, he took the $4,300 first prize and headed for Baton Rouge, the next Tour stop. His route took him near New Orleans where there was a track he was particularly fond of. He stayed for a couple of days and then proceeded on to Baton Rouge—without a red cent to his name.

ARNOLD PALMER

In 1991, Arnold Palmer came to Royal Birkdale for the British Open and checked into what was the best suite in the best hotel in the area. There was just one problem: through an oversight he had been given the suite that a young couple had reserved for their honeymoon.

The groom was beside himself. Not only would this cast a pall on the Great Day, but it was hardly the best way to start a marriage. The hotel management could offer the groom little hope that the situation would be resolved to his satisfaction, so he appealed directly to Palmer.

Not only did Palmer give up his suite, but he also stopped by and toasted the couple with champagne following that day's round.

Thousands, indeed tens of thousands, of golfers idolized Arnold Palmer. One who went on to a successful professional career was Roger Maltbie, who won five tournaments in his first eighteen years on tour and is

now an insightful golf commentator for NBC Sports.

Maltbie's first contact with Palmer came when he was eight years old. His parents had brought him to Pebble Beach for the Bing Crosby National Pro-Am.

When the Maltbies reached the second tee, Roger became separated from his parents and, lost in Palmer's enormous gallery, began to cry. Palmer heard him and walked over to the ropes, took him by the hand, and walked him down the middle of the fairway.

"Roger, get over here," called one of his parents from the gallery, certainly every bit as relieved as angry.

"Arnold has been my hero from that day on," says Maltbie.

Arnold Palmer came on tour at a time when Ben Hogan and Sam Snead were ending their domination of the professional game. Whereas the young Palmer was every bit a match for Snead's charisma, he couldn't begin to match Hogan's precision as a shotmaker. In fact, he was just the opposite. Where Hogan would take apart a course with surgical precision, Palmer would attack with abandon, often saving pars from impossible spots.

In one tournament Palmer missed a green and found himself down in a ditch with no real shot at the pin. As he studied his options, he spotted a friend, the sportswriter Jim Murray, in the gallery.

"You're always writing about Ben Hogan," said Palmer. "What would he do in a spot like this?"

"He wouldn't be in a spot like this," said Murray.

Having won the Masters in 1958 and 1960, Arnold Palmer was a favorite to defend his title in 1961. But after a 73 in the third round, he pretty much admitted defeat:

"Where's the casket?" he asked as he left the course and headed for the clubhouse.

It's safe to say that Arnold Palmer is one of the most, if not *the* most, recognizable golfers in the game's history, in no small part because of the amount of advertising he's appeared in over the years.

One of his most widespread and successful ad campaigns was for Pennzoil, in which he was featured driving an old tractor around a golf course. The commercials were so successful that people would bring cans of Pennzoil to tournaments and ask Arnold to autograph them—which he did, happily.

Another commercial called for Arnold to hit shots to a green that had been cleared of snow. It wasn't a long shot, but Arnold's ability to hit ball after ball onto the green impressed a member of the film crew, who had no idea whom he was watching.

"This guy is good," the technician said. "He's wasting his time being an actor. He should turn pro."

Arnold Palmer's father, Deacon, was a club professional, and even when Arnold was a youngster there was little doubt that he would follow in his father's footsteps. He worshiped his father and loved the game passionately.

Still, Arnold's mother wasn't sure that a pro's life, especially a tour pro in the 1950s, was a life she wanted for her son. Even after he won the 1954 U.S. Amateur at the Country Club of Detroit, she had serious misgivings. And she didn't feel any better after talking to Richard Tufts, a friend of the Palmer family who would go on to become president of the United States Golf Association.

"Mr. Tufts, I'm worried about Arnold," Mrs. Palmer confided. "I think he's going to turn pro after the Amateur."

"I'm sorry to hear that," said Tufts. "With a swing like that, he'll never make it on tour."

The U.S. Golf Association gave Arnold Palmer a special exemption from qualifying for the 1994 U.S. Open at Oakmont. Palmer had played in his first Open there, in his backyard, as a twenty-three-year-old amateur in 1953. The following year, he won the U.S. Amateur. Nine years later, in 1962, he again played in an Open at Oakmont, this time as the favorite. He lost in a playoff to Jack Nicklaus.

For Palmer, who won the Open in 1960 at Cherry Hills and finished second four times—three in playoffs—the emotion of the moment was heightened by the knowledge that the 1994 Open would be his last, and that it would be played before thousands of his most loyal fans.

In an inspired pairing, Palmer played with Rocco Mediate, a thirty-one-year-old tour pro who was born and raised near Pittsburgh and who idolized Palmer. As the two men came up the 18th hole at the close of the second round, it was clear that Palmer would miss the cut. The enormous gallery ringing the hole gave Palmer a standing ovation, and he responded by tipping his hat, smiling ruefully, and fighting back tears brought on by all the memories.

After putting out, Palmer and Mediate shook hands and embraced as the crowd's roar swelled again. At that moment Mediate, tears welling in his eyes, spoke for every one of his fellow players.

"You made all this possible," he said.

A few moments later, after signing his scorecard, Palmer was interviewed by ABC's Mark Rolfing. Rolfing was so choked up that he could barely ask his questions. Palmer could barely answer them.

What happened next is virtually unheard of in sports. Palmer was escorted into the interview area, which was jammed with writers, all of whom sensed they were witnessing an historic moment in golf. Many had known Palmer throughout his career and counted him as a friend. Some were mere infants when he won his first event on the regular Tour.

The room was still when Palmer began to speak.

"You all know pretty much how I feel. I have talked with most of you pretty much over the years . . ."

Finally, the emotion became too much. Tears filled Palmer's eyes and flowed down his face. He buried his face in a towel.

"I mean, it has been . . . well, you know, forty years of fun, work, and enjoyment. I haven't won that much . . . I've won a few tournaments . . . I've won some majors, but I suppose the most important thing is that . . . is that it has been as good as it has been to me."

He paused again to compose himself, and again put the towel to his face.

"I'm a little sun-whipped and tired, ready to take a rest. Hopefully there'll be a few more tournaments along the way. . . . That's about all I have to say. Thank you very much."

As Palmer got up to leave, the writers gave him a standing ovation. He made his way toward the exit, paused, and again covered his face with the towel, his back to the room. The ovation, which had ebbed, picked up and washed over Palmer again. Then he left, the most popular player in the history of the game. The most popular player who will ever play the game.

Rocco Mediate was right. He was the man who made it all possible.

BILLY JOE PATTON

Billy Joe Patton is probably best known as the amateur who dueled Ben Hogan and Sam Snead in the 1954 Masters. Playing in his first Masters, Patton led the tournament by a shot going into the 13th hole in the final round. His drive on that hole was OK, but only OK. He faced a tough decision with his second shot to the par 5. Should he lay up short of Rae's Creek or go for the green and possibly give himself a shot at an eagle?

While the enormous gallery cheered him on with shouts of "Go, Billy Joe. Go get 'em, Billy Joe," he decided to take a shot at the green.

"I didn't get this far by laying up," he said. "I'm not going to start now."

He should have. The ball went into Rae's Creek and Patton took a 7. He finished a shot behind Hogan and Snead, who played off the next day with Snead winning by a stroke.

Despite his loss Billy Joe Patton became something of a legend, nowhere more so than in his native South. This was particularly true at Pinehurst, where he was a fixture in the North and South Amateur, which he won three times.

One year Patton was in a playoff at Pinehurst with Dr. Bud Taylor, another fine player. After halving the first hole, Billy Joe's drive on the long, par-4 second settled on the lip of a fairway bunker. Another player, facing an awkward stance in the tall grass, would have properly decided to pitch the ball back into the fairway, but Billy Joe instinctively reached for a fairway wood, to the delight of the gallery.

As he stood over the ball, a car stopped on a nearby road and the driver—oblivious to what was going on—yelled, "Does anyone know where I can get a room?"

Billy Joe was nonplussed.

"If you wait a couple of minutes, you can probably have mine," he quipped.

Sure enough, a few minutes later the match ended when Dr. Taylor made a routine par.

HARVEY PENICK

For much of his long and distinguished teaching career, Harvey Penick was the best-kept secret in golf. The longtime professional at the Austin Country Club, he taught players as diverse as Ben Crenshaw, Tom Kite, Betsy Rawls, Kathy Whitworth, and Sandra Palmer—as well as thousands of weekend players who benefited from his wisdom, insights, and friendship.

Throughout his career, he kept a little red notebook filled with his thoughts and impressions. In 1991 he showed it to writer Bud Shrake and asked him if he thought there might be a book in it. Shrake instantly realized that not only was there a book there, but a classic. He approached Simon & Schuster, the publishing house, who offered a very healthy advance. Shrake reported the offer to Penick, who appeared crestfallen.

"I don't know, Bud," Penick said. "That's a lot of money, and I have a lot of medical bills to pay."

Shrake laughed and explained that S & S was going to pay *them* to write the book. Penick was stunned by the publisher's generosity, but it proved to be a wise investment: *Harvey Penick's Little Red Book* went on to become the biggest-selling sports book in history.

In 1994, NBC golf announcer Jim Lampley asked Harvey Penick if he would autograph a copy of his book for actor Jack Nicholson, Lampley's friend and golf partner. Lampley was somewhat taken aback when he realized that while Penick was more than happy to sign the book, he had no idea who Jack Nicholson was. When Penick was told that Nicholson was a highly acclaimed actor, he wrote: "Dear Jack—Congratulations: I understand you've had a good career. Harvey Penick."

PINE VALLEY GOLF CLUB

P ine Valley has long been considered one of the game's
most challenging and beautiful courses. It is a staple
on just about everyone's list of great courses, not only in
the United States but also around the world. Legend has
it that George Fazio, the longtime professional, would
often give the closing holes less than a full effort if it
meant shooting a good score, for fear of angering John
Arthur Brown, the club's autocratic president.

That's not to say that the course can't be had. One day
a 12-handicapper from out of town made the turn with a
50 on the front, which was nothing special. Then he
birdied five straight holes on the back and finished with
another birdie on 18—for one of the greatest 81s in golf
history.

The 145-yard, par-3 10th hole at Pine Valley would not be particularly difficult if it weren't for a treacherous pit bunker, the "Devil's Asshole," which guards the front of the green and catches not only tee shots that come up short but other shots from around the green that are misplayed.

Several years ago, a guest turned the front side in 42, a score far better than he dared expect. His tee shot on 10 carried to the back of the green—to his relief—but his birdie putt rolled off the green and into the bunker. Seven shots later it was still there. The disconsolate man put the ball into his pocket, sat down briefly on the edge of the bunker, broke into tears, and then walked back to the clubhouse.

A similar fate befell another man years later. He hit his drive into the bunker and, after a half-dozen vain attempts, elected to pitch back away from the green, where there is almost no lip to play over. This strategy would have been fine, except that he hit his next shot back into the bunker. He eventually settled for a 23 on the hole.

GARY PLAYER

When South Africa's Gary Player won the 1965 U.S. Open at Bellerive Country Club in St. Louis, he gave away his $25,000 first prize: $5,000 to help fight cancer and $20,000 to the U.S. Golf Association to help promote junior golf.

"That does it," said Bob Rosburg. "I always knew the USGA was tougher than cancer."

THE PRESS

Peter Thomson, the Australian who won five British Open championships, was playing in the 1957 St. Paul (Minnesota) Open. The course was laid out in such a manner that several holes were routed near a parking lot.

As Thomson, a man noted for a dry wit, was leaving one of the greens, he was approached by an eager young reporter covering his first tournament.

"Mr. Thomson, how was your round?" the reporter asked.

"Most satisfactory, considering I've only played two holes," Thomson said.

In 1971, the Golf Writers of America asked Argentina's Roberto de Vicenzo to present its Richardson Award, which he had won the year before, to longtime *New York Times* golf writer Lincoln Werden.

"I get this trophy, I think, because I signed the wrong scorecard a few years ago in the Masters. Mr. Werden, I think, gets this award for spelling my name wrong three times."

For many years a competition called "The Writer's Cup" was played between golf writers from the United States and those from Great Britain and Ireland. In the long and finest tradition of golf writers, it involved numerous freebies, very little journalism, a great deal of partying, and golf at some wonderful courses. One year the outing was particularly noteworthy, as much for what happened before a single shot was even struck as for the (dubious) quality of the golf. Peter Dobereiner, a long-time British golf writer and observer of the game, remembers.

"Well, the calamity began several weeks before, when one of the American writers, Larry Dennis, was preparing for the competition by practicing his golf swing in the luxurious confines of his living room," Dobereiner recalls. "He was quite gung-ho to win all the points for America, and as his finely calibrated swing had been idled all winter, it was clear that he dare not wait until he arrived in Ireland for the matches. Unfortunately, the act of watching her husband swing a golf club bored his poor wife into a stupor and she fell asleep, only to be awakened when Larry hit her foursquare on her foot, breaking every bloody bone in her ankle. I suspect it was the most solid contact Larry had made in some time.

"At any rate, Mr. and Mrs. Dennis, broken leg and all, arrived in Dublin for the next stage of the journey, which would serve as testimony to the ingenious nature of the Irish. The matches were to be played in Ballybunion on Monday, but through an oversight the writers were in Dublin on Sunday with no flights scheduled for Shannon. The people from the Irish Tourist Board devised what was really quite a clever solution: they arranged for the writers to board a special Air Lingus flight filled with people making a pilgrimage to Lourdes.

"The flight was in the air for just a few minutes when

the pilot announced that 'due to a small technical problem we shall have to set down in Shannon for just a few moments.' At the same time, the flight attendants went to all the writers and whispered that indeed the fix was in, and that when the plane arrived in Shannon, they should depart.

"The plane landed and the writers, including Mrs. Dennis, began to depart," Dobereiner recalls with a laugh. "One of the attendants, noticing the cast on her leg, pulled her aside and said quietly, 'Not you, darling. We're not quite to Lourdes yet.' "

The Masters has a tradition of welcoming writers from Great Britain and Ireland, and the spring sunshine and glorious flowers of Augusta are a welcome relief from the long, harsh North Atlantic winter.

One year a writer arrived at Boston's Logan Airport following a flight from London. His flight had been delayed, so when he got to the terminal he asked, "Excuse me, where do I get the plane to Augusta?" He got directions and raced off, barely making the plane on time. A short while later, the plane landed. It was a much shorter flight than he'd expected, as well it should have been since he had arrived in Augusta, Maine.

"Actually, I should have realized my error when the Atlantic was on the right side throughout the flight," he explained.

One of the British writers who regularly came to the Masters was Leonard Crawley, the golf correspondent of the *Daily Telegraph*. Crawley, an enormous man given to wearing red suits that matched his ruddy complexion and generous mustache, had been a Walker Cupper, a first-rank cricketer, and a superb marksman in his youth. For all his skills, Crawley was completely incapable of dealing with even the most basic of modern conveniences, including both the telephone and the typewriter—clearly a disadvantage for even the most talented journalist.

Still, such was Crawley's value that the *Telegraph* allowed him to hire a secretary to assist him wherever he went.

He arrived at Augusta to find that a lovely, young, shy—if conscientious—woman had been hired to assist him. Crawley was forthright in describing her responsibilities.

"Missy, your most important daily duty is to see that my cigar never goes out," he said, handing her a box of matches.

With that out of the way, Crawley set out for what he considered the most important part of a reporter's job—legwork—although in his case this was done largely in a sitting position in the convivial company of old friends.

After a particularly arduous afternoon of research and countless snifters of the club's finest brandies, Crawley fell into a much-deserved nap, his cigar clenched firmly between his teeth.

Well, this put his Missy in an awkward position. She wanted to do her job as instructed by the imperious Crawley, but were her nerves up to it? With trembling hands—as Crawley's fellow writers looked on in gleeful anticipation—she approached the cigar, flame in hand.

Alas, she missed the cigar and sent his brandy-sodden mustache into flames. Crawley awoke in a rage, and after he extinguished his face, sent Missy on her way, ending what might have been a most promising career in journalism.

⛳

In 1951, Leonard Crawley played a central role in one of the game's most celebrated matches. Like most writers, he was skeptical of the abilities of women golfers and the chances of their fledgling tour's surviving in America.

This, of course, put him on a collision course with Babe Zaharias, who issued a challenge to Crawley and his friends. She would assemble a team of women players and bring them to Wentworth, one of England's finest courses. There they would take on a team of Great Britian's six finest men amateurs. They would play from the championship tees. At stake was the honor of king and country, male dominance, and, last but certainly not least, Leonard Crawley's magnificent mustache, which he had offered to let Zaharias shave off if the unthinkable occurred.

The featured match pitted Crawley, an ex-Walker Cupper, against the Babe. Outdriving Crawley all day, she closed out the match 3 and 2.

And, in fact, the unthinkable did happen. The women won, 6½-2½, after sweeping every singles match.

Mercifully, the Babe let Crawley off, mustache intact.

⛳

No discussion of the golf press would be complete without a mention of "The Drummer." Bob Drum came to golf as a sportswriter for the *Pittsburgh Press*. He was primarily a baseball writer who was assigned to cover a kid from nearby Latrobe named Arnold Palmer.

"I went out to cover him in the Pennsylvania Junior and he lost in the first round," Drummer remembers. "If I had known he was going to grow up and become Arnold Palmer, I would have been nicer to the bum."

Be that as it may, Drummer's golf writing career took off when Palmer became the game's dominant player in the late 1950s and early 1960s. But in March 1961, with Palmer the defending champion at both the Masters and U.S. Open and the runner-up in the 1960 British Open, Drummer was diagnosed with cancer.

"The doctor told me this was a serious problem, and they wanted to cut me right away," says Drummer, now seventy-six. "I told him to forget it. I had to get down to Augusta. I told him we'd do it right after the Masters so I'd be fixed up in time for the Open at Oakland Hills in June.

"You'd think after all that I went through," says Drummer, "Arnold could have won at least one of them."

At the peak of Arnold Palmer's popularity, Pennsylvania's Republican party tried to talk him into running for governor. His wife, Winnie, was skeptical, to say the least.

"What is he going to do if he's asked a tough question?" she reportedly asked a friend—a question that speaks volumes about the regard in which golf writers held—and hold—Arnold Palmer.

Whatever excesses the American press might be guilty of, we pale in this regard by comparison with the British tabloids.

At the 1988 British Open at Royal Lytham and St. Anne's, Sandy Lyle was blithely making his way—as is his wont—toward the practice area when a topless woman leaped from the shrubs and threw her arms around him, just in time for a photographer from the tabs to snap his picture with one of the infamous "Page Three Girls."

The next morning, his wife greeted him with the paper and a short-but-to-the-point question.

"Well?"

"When Dan Jenkins was writing for *Sports Illustrated*, he'd kind of take it personally if Palmer or Nicklaus or one of the heroes didn't win the tournament he was covering," remembers Bob Drum. "In 1970, when Dave Stockton won the PGA Championship at Southern Hills, Dan spent most of his story writing about who didn't win, which was basically Arnold or Jack. You couldn't blame him. I mean, Stockton was this short-hitting guy who could putt and who nobody had heard of before. What was Dan supposed to do?

"Anyway, a couple of weeks later I'm at a tournament and Stockton comes into the pressroom," says the Drummer. "He's all upset and he says, 'Where's Jenkins? I want to talk to him.'

"Whom should I say is calling?" I asked him.

Bill Brendle, who died in 1982, was a longtime public relations guy for CBS Sports who, unlike a lot of publicists, was actually a good and helpful source. He was also quick with his American Express card—which sometimes got him into a little jam with his expense reports. More than once the bill arrived and he had to ask the waiter to "do me a favor and date this thing tomorrow. I already used up today last night."

During the 1994 British Open, writers scrambled to learn more about Jesper Parnevik, the young Swede who finished second.

"What is your father's name?" a writer asked.

"Bo," answered Parnevik.

"How do you spell it?" the writer asked.

"B.O.," he replied.

The British press has had an arm's-length relationship with Nick Faldo. It can be fairly said that Faldo has reciprocated in kind.

Early in his professional career, the tabloids referred to him as "Fold-O," for his inability to finish off a tournament.

Years later, after he had emerged as one of the game's dominant players, they still couldn't resist giving him a shot. During the 1994 British Open at Turnberry, Derek Lawrenson took him to task in *The Guardian* for his slow play:

"What could have possessed a hare to scamper across the 5th fairway just as Nick Faldo arrived?" he wrote. "Could it be that he recognized a tortoise when he saw one?"

A group of writers arranged to play at the Yale University Golf Course in New Haven. Their starting times were delayed by an NCAA women's tournament. As they waited, one of the writers noticed a woman driving by in a golf cart. He whistled and motioned her over.

"Are you the beer lady?" he asked.

"No, I'm the Yale coach," she replied as she drove away.

The Yale course is celebrated as a virtually pure example of architect Charles Blair MacDonald's work. Since it is an old course, it has a number of quirky characteristics, most notably blind drives and approaches.

After a round one glorious fall day, a friend asked Peter Andrews, the celebrated humorist and writer, what he thought of the course. Andrews had not had a particularly profitable day, and glumly gave his assessment of MacDonald's work.

"Eighteen good reasons to send a young man to Harvard," he growled.

A golf writer was flying from Germany to London, and as the plane began its approach to Heathrow, suddenly the lights of the city went black. The plane was forced to circle while waiting for the lights to return. After a few minutes, the pilot came on the loudspeaker with what was supposed to be a comforting announcement.

"Ladies and gentlemen, this is your pilot speaking," he said in a clipped German accent. "You have nothing to be concerned about. There are no pilots in the world with more experience flying over a blacked-out London than the German pilots of Lufthansa."

JACKIE PUNG

Almost every golfer knows the story of Roberto de Vicenzo, who lost the 1968 Masters when he signed an incorrect scorecard. Less known is the story of Jackie Pung and the 1957 U.S. Women's Open at Winged Foot's East Course.

Pung lost the 1953 Women's Open to Betsy Rawls in a playoff, 77-70. But four years later she appeared, at least until the last minute, to have won the most important title in women's golf.

After finishing the final round with a 72, it was determined that she had signed an incorrect scorecard. The 72 was correct, but the card had her down for a 6 instead of a 5 on the 6th hole. Under the Rules of Golf, the U.S. Golf Association had no choice but to disqualify her.

The members of Winged Foot, in a remarkable gesture, decided to do what they could to make it up to her. They took up a collection and raised $3,000 as a consolation prize. That may not sound like much these days, until you consider that the winner—Betsy Rawls—took home a first-prize check of just $1,800.

TED RAY

E ngland's Ted Ray was one of the game's dominant players in the early part of this century, winning both a U.S. Open and a British Open. Oddly, he is perhaps best known in America for joining Francis Ouimet and Harry Vardon in the celebrated playoff for the 1913 U.S. Open at The Country Club in Brookline, Massachusetts.

However, it could have easily been a four-way playoff if not for the aftereffects of a heated political debate between Ray and fellow Englishman Wilfred Reid on the eve of the final round.

Ray, a great bear of a man, got into a raging argument with the 130-pound Reid over some matter related to English politics. Reid angered Ray to the point that Ray lunged at him, punching him in the head and almost knocking him out.

Reid was tied for the lead going into the final round, but he shot himself out of any chance for the title. Ray made it to the playoff, but shot an uninspired 78 and lost by six shots to Ouimet.

BOB ROSBURG

Bob Rosburg was a member of Stanford University's golf team in the 1940s. At the time, collegiate golf was far more low-key than it is today. In fact, as Rossie puts it, "Our idea of a road trip was going to San Francisco.

"In 1946, the university told us that if we won the conference championship they'd pay our way to the NCAAs," Rosburg remembers. "When we won the conference they changed their mind, so we had to raise the money ourselves. When we won the NCAAs, they made a big deal about how proud they were and they wanted to put the trophy on display. We wouldn't let them. We put it in the window of a clothing store downtown."

DONALD ROSS

Donald Ross came to America from Scotland and quickly established himself as one of the premier golf course architects—a man whose works are revered today, and many of which are the standards against which others are measured.

Ross was fiercely proud of his work and not above promoting his efforts. He once telegraphed a player following a tournament at one of his courses, congratulating him on winning.

"Excellent. The greatest," reads Ross's cable.

"Undeserving of such praise," the player wired back.

"Was referring to the course," Ross replied.

"So was I," the player shot back.

THE ROYAL AND ANCIENT GOLF CLUB OF ST. ANDREWS

For much of its early history, the Old Course at St. Andrews was closed on Sundays. One day a gentleman arrived and was miffed when he learned that he couldn't play. He got into a discussion with Old Tom Morris, the club's professional. After a few minutes, Morris had heard enough.

"Look, sir, the Old Course needs a rest, even if you don't," he said. "There'll be no golf played here today."

THE RULES

A rules official at the North and South Women's Amateur at Pinehurst faced a difficult, if not impossible, rules decision.

An elderly matriarch, well into her seventies, picked up on a hole. Since it was a stroke-play tournament, the rules called for her disqualification. But she was in the last flight, with no chance of winning, so the official offered to make a deal.

"If you won't tell anyone, I won't either," he said. "Just give yourself a double bogey."

"I won't do any such thing," she huffed. "I insist on being penalized."

The official explained that the proper penalty called for disqualification.

"That's absurd," she replied.

The official tried another tack. He offered to penalize her two strokes.

"Too much," she said. "I'll take one stroke, young man, and I have no intention of standing here quibbling with you any further."

One stroke it was.

In an earlier tournament at Pinehurst, a player's ball came to rest in the cuff of a spectator's pants. An official ruled that the ball must be played as it lay—a rather Calvinist interpretation of the rules even then.

The player was willing to give it a shot, so to speak, but the spectator would have no part of it. Scanning the gallery to make sure there were no ladies present, he carefully pulled off his pants and held them out so the golfer could play his shot. The shot was successful, the spectator put his pants back on, and both men received a much-deserved ovation.

THE RYDER CUP

This biennial series of matches between professionals from the United States and Europe began in 1927. While the Americans have dominated the matches for most of its history, recently the Europeans have shown considerable strength with the emergence of players like Seve Ballesteros, Nick Faldo, Bernard Langer, and Ian Woosnam. Today it is one of the most popular events in golf, and one with a rich history.

In 1971, the Ryder Cup matches were held at Old Warson in St. Louis. One of the most imaginative pairings was that uniting Ireland's Christy O'Connor with England's Neil Coles. They were teamed in the lead foursomes match against Billy Casper and Miller Barber.

Foursomes, or alternate shot, requires a higher degree of strategy than four-ball or individual play. Of vital importance is deciding which player will drive on the even-numbered holes and which will drive on the odd-numbered holes. For example, if three of the par 3s are even-numbered holes, you'd want the stronger iron player to drive on those holes.

Knowing that if he and O'Connor could lead off with a win it would inspire their teammates, Coles was anxious to learn which holes he would be driving on. This would help him prepare mentally for the round. At dinner that night he asked O'Connor—known far and wide as simply "Himself"—what the order would be.

"It's no matter, really," said O'Connor. "We'll think about it on the overnight."

The next morning at breakfast, Coles asked again.

"Well, I have been thinking about it," said Himself.

"And . . . ," said Coles.

"And I'm still thinking," Himself said. "You're right, though. It is a vitally important question."

By the time they finally reached the first tee, O'Connor had very nearly exhausted himself with his thinking. Suddenly, the answer came to him.

"I know, Neil," he said. "We'll flip for it."

So they did, and went on to beat the Americans, 2 and 1.

The 1973 Ryder Cup matches were played at Muirfield in Scotland, where, a year earlier, Lee Trevino had won his second British Open championship. Naturally, this gave Trevino—then at the height of his game—considerable confidence in his Sunday-morning singles match against young Peter Oosterhuis.

"If I can't beat Peter Oosterhuis, I'll kiss the American team's asses," said Trevino.

Well, Oosterhuis proved surprisingly tough and the

match ended in a tie. Somewhere, it is rumored, there is a picture of the American team standing in a line, facing away from the camera, with their pants dropped to their ankles, waiting for Trevino to make good on his promise.

In 1949, the Ryder Cup matches were played on British soil for the first time since the end of World War II. The country was still reeling from the effects of the war, and the Americans elected to bring their own food with them rather than take their chances with what might be available in England.

By any standard, their menus were impressive. The supplies included twelve sides of ribs, twelve hams, twelve boxes of bacon, and literally hundreds of steaks.

To put it mildly, this display didn't sit well with some of the British, who felt it was yet another example of American excess.

As a rule, the Ryder Cup matches have been models of sportsmanship. But the 1969 match at Royal Birkdale also showed the players at their worst.

The matches will best be remembered for Jack Nicklaus's decision to concede a short putt on the final hole to Tony Jacklin, ensuring a tie. But early in the week the atmosphere was decidedly less sportsmanlike.

The bad blood began when the British captain, Eric Brown, was quoted as saying that while he liked Americans well enough off the course, when on the course he "hated them and wanted to massacre them." Further, he instructed his players not to help look for the Americans' balls if they were lost in the deep, thick roughs.

In the first morning's foursomes, Lee Trevino was paired with Ken Still against Maurice Bembridge and Bernard Gallacher. The match was very close, and on the 13th tee tensions exploded when Bembridge asked Still not to move, claiming it was distracting him and implying that Still was doing it intentionally.

Not only did Still move out of Bembridge's vision, but he ordered all the caddies and officials to do the same. Still's mood didn't improve when, a few minutes later, Trevino's approach shot plugged under the lip of a bunker. Still tried to explode the ball out, but it bounced back and hit him on the shoulder.

"Did it hit you?" Trevino asked.

Still didn't answer.

"Pick it up," said Trevino, conceding the hole. The Americans went on to lose, 2 and 1.

Ken Still was involved in more disputes in later matches. Paired with Dave Hill in a match against Bernard Gallacher and Brian Huggett, the four went at it continuously. On the first green, both Americans had to be asked to remain still. On the next hole, just as Huggett was preparing to putt, Still ordered his caddie not to attend the flagstick.

By the 7th hole, the situation had gotten so bad that the team captains, Eric Brown and Sam Snead, had to try to cool things off. When Gallacher claimed that Still had putted out of turn, Still snatched his opponent's marker, tossed it to him, and said, "You can have your putt, the hole, and the goddamned Cup." The emotionalism of the match inspired Hill, who unleashed his formidable shotmaking skills and led the Americans to a 2 and 1 win. Alas, even the match's conclusion didn't mark the end of the problems. That night, Still and Huggett got into an argument outside the restaurant of the Prince of Wales hotel.

However, the matches ended on a positive note. Hill later asked Huggett to join him for a practice round in an upcoming tournament. And Nicklaus's decision to give Jacklin his putt on 18 is still considered one of the game's greatest acts of sportsmanship.

GENE SARAZEN

In the early 1930s, Gene Sarazen took part in a test to establish just how fast a golf ball came off the face of a driver.

Sarazen went to a Detroit automobile testing ground and stood near the straightaway of an oval track. As a race car came down the track, a scientist signaled Sarazen to hit the ball at the moment the car passed him. Naturally, it took a number of tries, but the officials finally selected five attempts on which Sarazen had timed his shot nearly perfectly.

The conclusion was that the ball came off the clubface faster than the 120 miles per hour that the car was traveling. The five drives averaged 230 yards, and the car caught up to the ball in slightly over 115 yards, which indicated just how much the ball slowed in flight. On average, it took Sarazen's shots 4.5 seconds to carry the 230 yards, whereas it took the car 4.1 seconds.

Did the experiment actually prove anything?

Of course, the methods used were not very scientific and the test was therefore subject to a certain amount of individual interpretation. But the experiment did pick up a lot of headlines for golf, which is one of the things that Sarazen did best for the game throughout his career.

In 1973, the fiftieth anniversary of his first visit to the Open, seventy-one-year-old Gene Sarazen traveled to Royal Troon for the British Open. Sarazen came to the short, par-3 8th hole—the "Postage Stamp"—in the first round and aced it. The next day he made a 2.

Gene Sarazen and his longtime friend Fred Corcoran were in the clubhouse at Augusta National watching the telecast of the 1976 Masters. When Jack Nicklaus hit his 4-iron approach to the 15th green—the site of Sarazen's famous double eagle in 1935—it looked as if the ball might roll into the hole.

"Go in! Go in!" urged Sarazen.

Corcoran grabbed him by the arm.

"Quiet, Gene," he said. "The double eagle is your last claim to fame."

Sarazen's double eagle was arguably the most famous shot in Masters history, but that didn't stop Augusta National chairman Clifford Roberts from taking him to task when he committed what Roberts considered an unpardonable sin. For his appearance on a "Shell's Wonderful World of Golf" filmed in Ireland, Sarazen thought it would be nice to wear something green—something, say, like a Masters green jacket.

When Roberts heard about this he was furious, and chastised Sarazen the next time they talked. Today, the rules are clear-cut. The reigning Masters champion can take the jacket off-site for one year. After that, he can wear the green jacket only at Augusta National.

In the 1931 Ryder Cup matches at Scioto Country Club, in Columbus, Ohio, Gene Sarazen faced Fred Robson in a final-day singles match. On a short par 3, Robson's shot came to rest twenty-five feet from the hole. Sarazen's tee shot flew over the green and into a nearby refreshment stand, coming to rest in a crack in the cement floor. Robson, who was struggling against Sarazen, surely thought this break would mark a change in his fortunes. At best, Sarazen would make a bogey. He might even be forced to concede the hole.

As Robson waited on the green, Sarazen studied the situation. At the last minute, he and his caddie moved a refrigerator out of the way. He lined up his shot, hit down sharply on the ball, and watched as it rocketed through a tiny window, landed on the green, and rolled to a stop ten feet from the hole.

It was more than Robson could stand. Shaken, he three-putted for a bogey and lost the hole to Sarazen's par. The match ended, not surprisingly, with a 7 and 6 Sarazen win.

Gene Sarazen won the 1922 U.S. Open and was heavily favored to win the PGA Championship a few months later at Oakmont. In fact, he did, but he was almost disqualified before hitting a shot.

He had played an exhibition in Ohio and was having dinner in a Columbus restaurant. A man came in and asked him what he was doing there when he was supposed to play his first match at nine the next morning.

Sarazen didn't waste a minute. While his friends paid the check, he raced to the train station and scrambled aboard a train as it pulled away from the station. Unfortunately, the train was late getting into Pittsburgh, and by the time Sarazen got to the course, it was two hours past his starting time. Today, he would have automatically been disqualified, but the PGA let him play. He wound up winning, beating Emmet French, 4 and 3, in the final.

After winning the 1922 U.S. Open, Gene Sarazen agreed to attend a huge party in his honor. The party got underway without him, and his friends began to worry that something untoward might have happened to him. Soon, however, the lights dimmed and a spotlight was focused on an enormous, papier-mâché golf ball that was carted into the ballroom.

As a band struck up "The Star-Spangled Banner," Sarazen, who was crouching inside the ball, rose through the top of the ball holding the U.S. Open trophy aloft and waving to the crowd, which roared its approval.

Playing the 18th hole in the Masters one year, Gene Sarazen hit his approach over the green, and the ball rolled under the long, flowing skirt of a woman seated on the ground behind the green. As Sarazen made his way up the fairway a rules official, Ike Grainger, asked the woman to stand so Sarazen could play the shot. Amid much laughter from the people around her, she stood, but the ball was nowhere to be found.

"Madam, do you suppose you could do something to help us find the ball? Otherwise, Mr. Sarazen will be forced to play it as it lies," Grainger said.

By now, Sarazen had made it to the green and was looking on as the woman began shaking and shimmying. Finally, the ball fell from one of the folds of her skirt. Sarazen thanked her, took a club, and pitched it stiff—to the delight of the crowd and the relief of the woman.

"SHELL'S WONDERFUL WORLD OF GOLF"

"In 1967, we were filming a match in Germany between Jay Hebert and Freidel Schmaderer, who, while he was probably the best player in Germany at the time, was no Bernhard Langer," remembers Fred Raphael, the creative genius behind the popular, long-running program. "Jay was delayed getting over to Europe, so we found ourselves with a few days to kill. Gene Sarazen, who was then in his sixties, offered to play Freidel for dinner that night. Gene won pretty easily. He beat him again the next day and the following day as well. Freidel began to get worried.

" 'This Hebert, he's not better than Mr. Sarazen, yes?' he asked me.

" 'Oh no, just younger,' I assured him.

"Anyway, Jay finally arrived, but he was dead tired and his play showed it," Raphael recalls. "He was getting killed, so I did something I never did before or since in the series. I told everyone we had to quit filming for the day because the light was bad. In fact, the light was perfect, and Freidel kept looking up at the sky trying to figure out how it could possibly be any better. We came back the next day, and Jay won pretty easily. In fact, he had so much fun over in Europe that he asked if he could stay around for the filming of the next show, in Copenhagen. I said sure, so we paid him $35 a day to be a part of the gallery."

"We were filming a show in France one year and had to use a crew that didn't speak much, if any, English," recalls Fred Raphael. "I knew we were in trouble when I asked one of the cameramen if he was able to follow the flight of the ball.

" 'Oui, Monsieur Fred,' he said with this huge smile on his face.

"On the next hole I asked him if he'd missed the ball, and he smiled just as widely and said, 'Oui, Monsieur Fred.' "

"People sometimes said the players really didn't care all that much about winning, but that's not true," remembers Raphael. "I remember one match in particular. It was in Panama, and Chi Chi Rodriguez lost to Mike Souchak. Chi Chi really wanted to win, I think, because it would have meant a lot to the local golfers. When he lost, he was so upset he forgot to take off his spikes before he drove to the airport. Of course, he also forgot to pick up his wife and daughter at the clubhouse."

Weather is always a concern when it comes to a televised golf event, but it proved to be a particular problem in a "Shell's Wonderful World of Golf" match at Banff Springs in Canada between Jackie Burke, Jr., and Stan Leonard. Because of snow, the match took a full week to film.

SHINNECOCK
HILLS GOLF CLUB

S hinnecock, located on the eastern end of New York's
Long Island, was one of the founding clubs of the
U.S. Golf Association. It hosted the second U.S. Open in
1896; in 1986, it hosted the Open for just the second
time. That year, Raymond Floyd shot an inspired final
round to edge Lanny Wadkins and Chip Beck. The Open
will return in 1996, to the delight of players and purists
who regard the course as one of the world's finest tests.

How good is Shinnecock?

"I knew as soon as I played my first practice round that
I could win the Open at Shinnecock," said Raymond
Floyd. "It's a pure golf course. There's nothing that
anyone can do to trick it up. It's perfect as it is."

That Shinnecock's membership has traditionally been
drawn from the swellest of New York's society swells
never had much of an impact on its longtime professional, Charles Thom, an immigrant from Scotland.

Thom served as pro from 1905 to 1966, and stayed around as pro emeritus until his death at age ninety-eight.

He once dismissed a particularly influential member as a man who "couldn't find his ass with both hands if you gave him a one-hand head start."

On another occasion, Thom watched a foursome flail their way through the tall grass that separates the 9th and 18th holes. After a few minutes, he couldn't take it any longer.

"I don't know where you think you're going," he shouted down the hill from the clubhouse, "but you sure as hell need a new map."

But Thom is best remembered for his frustration as he tried to teach a wealthy Wall Street speculator how to play. The man proved to be every bit as inept as he was enthusiastic. He was willing to pay Thom any amount of money for lessons if only he could become respectable on the golf course. It didn't take Thom long to realize that there might not be enough money in the world to get the job done.

One day, Thom blurted out in exasperation: "You'll make this a lot easier on both of us if you'll just keep your mind on the ball instead of your damned money."

Shinnecock's rambling clubhouse was designed by the famous New York architect Sanford White. White is almost as well known for his death as for the exquisite quality of his work.

White, a fixture of New York society, was having dinner with a Broadway showgirl, Evelyn N. Thaw, when her husband walked in, pulled a revolver, and fired three rounds into White, killing him.

The killer, a millionaire named Harry K. Thaw, was sentenced to seven years in an "asylum for the criminally insane." The hardship of the sentence was lessened by the fact that his time was spent in his own lavishly decorated suite of rooms.

Upon his release, Thaw traveled to Florida for the winter. There, he was exposed to the work of an architect whose Spanish-inspired motifs were particularly garish and jarring.

On his first day in Florida, Thaw is reported to have looked around in shock and revulsion and exclaimed, "My God, I killed the wrong architect."

J. C. SNEAD

J. C. Snead is best known as Sam's nephew, but he's an accomplished golfer in his own right. His sport of choice was baseball, at which he was good enough to land on a farm team of the old Washington Senators before turning pro and joining the Tour. He won eight times on tour, but his best chance to win the prestigious Players Championship was literally blown away one year.

"I was paired with J.C. when the tournament was played on the original Sawgrass course," remembers Tom Watson. "The wind was unbelievable. Signs were being blown down. We came to 17 and J.C. was in contention. The hole was playing straight downwind, which made it almost impossible to hold the ball on the green. You weren't even thinking about getting it close to the hole, which was cut on the top level of the three-tiered green.

"Well, J.C. hit the most beautiful little shot in there that you've ever seen. We were all watching the ball get close to the hole when the wind gusted and knocked J.C.'s hat off. The hat started rolling and flip-flopping down the fairway. Pretty soon it was getting near the green. It was like watching an accident in slow motion. You knew what was going to happen next, but you couldn't believe it. The hat reached the green, rolled up all three levels, and hit J.C.'s ball. He had to take a penalty stroke, because the hat counted as part of his equipment. It's still the most unlucky thing I've ever seen on a golf course."

SAM SNEAD

There have been players who were Sam Snead's equal in the record books, but you'd be hard-pressed to find anyone who was his equal working or controlling the ball. He could fade it or draw it, hit it high and land it soft or bring it in low and running, to keep it out of the wind. He was, quite simply, a genius who combined superb technical skills with a sheer love of competition.

Sam will go down in golf history side by side with Ben Hogan, his greatest rival. A player once asked Sam why he would so often shoot at pins that Hogan and others would play away from. Anyone looking for a cosmic discussion of course strategy would have been disappointed by the simplicity of Sam's answer.

"That's what pins are there for," Sam said.

Early in his career Sam was paired with the Scotsman Willie MacFarlane, the man who beat Bobby Jones in a playoff to win the 1925 U.S. Open Championship. Sam was just making a name for himself on tour at the time, and when MacFarlane noticed he was paying careful attention to MacFarlane's club selection, he decided to teach the youngster a lesson.

They came to a par 3, and MacFarlane took his time selecting a club, making sure that Sam saw exactly which club he pulled. When the time came to play the shot, he "dead-handed" it—that is, took something off his shot. The ball came to rest just under the hole for a birdie putt.

Sam pulled the same club for his drive, knocking the ball over the green.

"My boy," said MacFarlane as they walked to the green. "Never go to school on another man's club, or ye'll never make a penny in this game."

Sam had a tendency to rely heavily on caddies for club selection, sometimes to his detriment. But in Jimmy Steed, a caddie from Pinehurst, he found someone with an uncanny ability to pick the right club. That added confidence made Sam even more awesome than usual.

Sam reasoned that if he could have Jimmy caddie for him in the U.S. Open, he'd finally break through and win the one major title that had eluded him. There was only one problem: the USGA required players to use local caddies in the Open.

Still, Sam thought he had a solution. A year before the 1956 Open at Oak Hill, he arranged for Jimmy to move to Rochester, New York. It was a nice try, but just prior to the start of the Open Joe Dey, the secretary of the USGA, ruled that even though Jimmy had lived in Rochester for almost a year, he wasn't a local caddie.

"I've had some pretty interesting caddies over the years, but one of the tops was O'Bryant Williams, who used to caddie for me at Augusta," Sam remembers. "He was a hell of a character. Had about eighteen or so kids. And he was a good caddie, except you couldn't count on his clubbing you. He'd be all right most of the time, but sometimes you'd wonder what the hell he was thinking about. In 1949, when I won the Masters for the first time, I got so fed up with it, I told him, 'O'Bryant, if I ever ask you what club to use, you just say I don't know. That's all. Just say, "Sam, I don't know." You don't need to make any excuses. Just say you don't know.'

"Well, the weather was tough that year, and in one round we got to the 6th tee and the wind's a-howlin' and it's just as cold as can be. Old O'Bryant was just miserable. He was standing there holding my bag and shivering away. Now, the key to that hole is the wind, just like at number 12. It can trick you and send you off to a big number. I asked him, 'O'Bryant, which way was the wind blowing yesterday?'

" 'I ain't talking, Mr. Sam,' he said.

"I told him, 'O'Bryant, I'm not asking you what club to use. I just want to know what the hell way the wind was blowing yesterday.'

"He said, 'I know what you're up to, and you ain't gonna give me hell. I'm not talking.'

"And you know what? He didn't."

O'Bryant was on Snead's bag five years later when Snead beat Ben Hogan, 70-71, in a playoff capping what Bob Jones later called one of the "most memorable Masters."

"O'Bryant was what you'd call excitable," Sam remembers. "He'd be pullin' real hard for you, and not just because of the money. I had this one long putt and O'Bryant was tending the flag. As the ball got up a rise and headed towards the hole, it looked like it might come up short. O'Bryant set to wavin' on the ball, trying to help it get to the hole. He damned near hit the ball. Lucky for him he didn't, and it went in the hole.

"As we walked to the next tee, I told him, 'O'Bryant, it's a damn good thing you didn't touch that ball. I'd have buried you right in this green—and the last thing it needs is one more big hump.' "

With the passage of time it's easy to forget what an awesome player Sam was in his prime, or even in his early days on tour. The long-sleeve shirts he wore in the 1930s would routinely shred at the shoulder seams from the sheer force of his swing.

In the 1936 Hershey Open, Gene Sarazen watched Sam hit one 300-yard drive after another. After his round, the writers asked Sarazen what he thought.

"I've just seen a kid who doesn't know the first thing about golf," Sarazen said. "And I don't want to be playing when he learns."

Sam didn't know it at the time, but he played a pivotal role in Harvey Penick's decision to abandon full-time tournament play and focus on teaching.

"I was playing in the Houston Open one year and the players were all talking about this fellow from the Virginia mountains," Penick said one day. "They said they'd never seen anyone hit the ball quite like him. I went over to take a look. They were right. Not only had I never seen a ball hit like that, I'd never heard a shot sound like it did when Sam hit it. It came off the clubface with a crack, like a rifle shot. At that moment, I decided that the life of a teaching professional looked pretty good to me."

Sam came to Pinehurst for the 1938 North and South Open and played very well in the first round, only to be disqualified for signing an incorrect scorecard.

Disconsolate, he went to a drugstore in the village to get something from the soda fountain. As he walked through the door, he noticed a slot machine and decided to try to change his luck. He put a nickel in the machine and pulled the handle. So much change came cascading out that he couldn't hold it all, and he had to have help picking the coins up off the floor.

In 1946, at the urging of his sponsors, Wilson Sporting Goods, Sam traveled to St. Andrews for the first British Open played following the war.

Postwar Scotland and Sam were not an ideal pairing. The weather was cold and damp. The Old Course was unlike anything he'd ever seen before. The Scottish burr was alien to Sam, who grew up in Virginia's mountains. The food was barely tolerable and, as a final insult, his prize for winning the oldest championship in the game came to a mere $600 in American money. The trip to Scotland had cost him almost $2,000.

After the awards ceremony, a British writer asked Sam if he'd be back to defend his title the following year at Hoylake.

"Are you kidding?" Sam said in disbelief.

Sam always enjoyed playing as long as there was a little money riding on the match. It didn't have to be much, just enough to hold his interest. Otherwise, he often said, he'd "rather be out fishing."

He had a reputation as a hustler, but nothing could be further from the truth. He'd always give people their handicap, properly figuring that just playing the Great Sam Snead was enough to throw anyone off their game.

Although he won most of his friendly matches, he did lose on occasion. In one case, it cost him $20. At the match's conclusion, he reached into his pocket and handed his opponent a $20 bill.

"Sam, do me a favor and autograph it for me," the man said.

"What for?" Sam asked.

"I want to take it home, frame it, and put it on my office wall," the man said. "Otherwise, nobody will believe I beat you."

"Here, give me that $20," Sam said, taking the bill back from the man. "I'll give you a check."

Sam joined the Tour in 1937 and almost won the first U.S. Open he played in—that year's Open at Oakland Hills.

After finishing the final round he went to the clubhouse, where he ran into Tommy Armour.

"Congratulations, laddie," said Armour. "You've won your Open."

The writers surrounded Snead, forgetting that Ralph Guldahl was still on the course with a chance of catching the young Virginian.

"I don't know, fellas," said Sam. "Goldie's out there, and all he needs is a couple of birdies to win. I don't want to jinx myself."

Jinx or not, Guldahl did what he had to do, making two birdies on the last six holes to win.

"After Goldie made that putt you could have fired a shotgun off in the locker room and not hit anyone but me," said Sam. "That's how fast the newspaper boys cleared out of there."

Guldahl, for his part, remains something of a mystery man. Between 1937 and 1939, he won back-to-back U.S. Opens, a Masters, and three Western Opens—at that time considered on a par with any of the major championships. At that point in his career Guldahl was considered far superior to fellow Texans Ben Hogan and Byron Nelson.

But after winning four times in 1939, Guldahl's game left him. He would win only two other tournaments before retiring from the Tour in 1950.

Some people think his problems on the course stemmed from his agreeing to write an instruction book after winning the Masters. The legend is that the book project forced him to think about swing mechanics for the first time, and that he suffered paralysis through analysis.

If so, he wasn't the first. Nor the last.

$\text{\textcircled{\scriptsize{\%}}}$

Another memorable Snead match came in the finals of the 1938 PGA Championship at Shawnee-on-Delaware, where he faced the diminutive Paul Runyan and lost, 8 and 7.

There's a temptation to paint this match as a classic "David vs. Goliath" upset, but in truth Runyan was one of the game's best players, having already won the 1934 PGA in a playoff over Craig Wood—the year Runyan was the leading money winner. Snead, for his part, was twenty-six years old and in only his second year on tour. Although he often outdrove Runyan by as much as forty yards, Runyan was a genius from 100 yards in—as good as anyone who ever played the game. And in match play—as the PGA was set up in those days—that gave Runyan a huge psychological advantage. A case in point:

"We came to this one hole and Sam had laid a perfect stymie on me," said Runyan. "His ball was two feet from the hole, on exactly the same line as my ball, which was a foot further out. Back then this meant that I had to pitch the ball over Sam's ball, which was a daunting shot to say the least. I'm sure Sam realized it was. But I was very confident in that shot. I hit it, the ball flew over Sam's ball, bounced once, and went into the hole. I quickly walked over, picked my ball out of the cup, rolled

Sam's ball back towards his feet, and headed for the next tee. I'm not sure that was the turning point in the match, but it was certainly one of them."

It's true that Runyan won, 8 and 7, but it's unlikely that the results would have been different if it had been medal play. "Little Poison," as he was known, was 24 under par for the 94 holes they played.

That's tough to beat. Even for a Sam Snead.

Sam Snead's 1954 playoff victory over Ben Hogan in the Masters might well go down as his greatest win in a major championship. Not only were the two men the best players in the world at that time, but it also marked the last time Sam won a major.

How memorable was it?

Forty years later, Sam can remember every shot he hit, every shot Hogan hit, and where every pin was placed. In fact, sometimes when people present him with scorecards from Augusta National for his autograph, he writes down both players' scores and signs the card, "Sam Snead, 1954 Masters."

In 1950, Sam Snead was at the height of his considerable powers. He won eleven tournaments that year, including a playoff against Ben Hogan in the Los Angeles Open, Hogan's first tournament since his near-fatal automobile accident. Snead also won the Vardon trophy with a scoring average for the year of 69.23—the lowest in history.

For his part, Hogan won the U.S. Open at Merion in a dramatic playoff with Lloyd Mangrum and George Fazio.

When the nation's golf writers voted for "Player of the Year" honors, the award went to Ben Hogan.

"I was never the same after that," said Snead. "It took the wind out of my sails and I never really cared all that much about winning again."

Of course, he did go on to win many more times. In fact, he became the oldest man to win a Tour event when he won the 1965 Greater Greensboro Open at age fifty-two—the seventh time he won that tournament.

Snead had gone to Greensboro to attend a dinner in his honor, and decided to play only at the urging of tournament officials, who knew his appearance would help attract larger crowds.

"I don't figure to win, but you never can tell," Snead said at the dinner. "If I get a few breaks, those boys better watch out."

He didn't need many breaks. He shot a four-round total of 273 to beat Billy Casper, Phil Rodgers, and Jack McGowen by a staggering five shots.

Not surprisingly, young players could find Sam Snead an intimidating player to deal with. Not that he tried to be brusque or tough, but he was, after all, one of the game's greatest players.

When Bob Toski joined the Tour in the 1950s, he was in awe of Snead's game, particularly his skill in the bunkers—for which he's always been underrated.

"I knew I couldn't just go up and ask him for a lesson, but I also knew that he wouldn't turn down a bet," remembers Toski. "I used to bet him milk shakes that I could get ten balls closer to the hole than he could. I hardly ever beat him, at least at first, but I learned to be a pretty good bunker player just by watching Sam. I paid for a lot of milk shakes, but it was the best investment I ever made."

It was Snead who gave the diminutive Toski his nickname "Mouse."

"He saw me walking through the locker room on my way to the showers," Toski remembers. "He said, 'Mouse, you better tie a rope around you before you go in there. You might slide right through those little drains.' "

Tom Kite was another player who took advantage of Sam's competitive instincts to become a better player.

"Sam was still playing a fair amount on tour when I came out in 1972," Kite remembers. "I introduced myself and asked if I could play with him in his practice rounds. We didn't play for much, just enough to keep his interest, but it was an education that I couldn't have gotten any other way. I remember going back home to Austin and asking Harvey Penick, my teacher, whether it was possible for a player to develop all the shots Sam had and then hit them in competition. Mr. Penick disappointed me a little by saying 'probably not.' But he was right."

Many—in fact, most—of Sam's acts of kindness to other players have gone unreported, but here's a good example of his generosity.

He was paired with Johnny Miller in the 1974 Los Angeles Open. It was the year Miller broke through and became a dominant player, winning eight times and ending the year as the Tour's leading money winner. But in Los Angeles, he wasn't in contention and wasn't very interested in being there. As the two men walked together down one of the final holes, Sam decided to give Miller some advice.

"Look, Johnny, I wouldn't say this if I didn't think you're a good guy," Sam said. "These people paid good money to come out here and see you play your best. This round may not mean much to you, but it means a lot to them. You're going to be a great player, and it would be a shame if you got a reputation for dogging it. You owe it to these people and you owe it to yourself."

That night Sam got a phone call in his hotel room. It was Johnny Miller thanking him for the advice.

♦

Despite winning more tournaments than any man alive, people always point to Sam's failure to win the U.S. Open as a flaw in his career—just as they always note that Arnold Palmer never won the PGA Championship, which, because Palmer's father was a club professional, was a tournament particularly close to his heart.

But consider this: if he had shot 69 or better in the final round, Sam Snead would have won nine U.S. Opens. And how would that have changed the debate over who was the greatest golfer of all time?

♦

LEFTY STACKHOUSE

There are players with tempers. There are players with fierce tempers. Then there is Lefty Stackhouse, who was the standard all others are held against.

He came to one tournament and noticed that True Temper, the shaft manufacturer, had sent a representative out with a set of clubs fitted with their latest shaft. Lefty asked the man if he might borrow the clubs for a practice round. The man, apparently not aware of Lefty's reputation, thought it might help promote the shafts.

Wrong.

A few hours later, Stackhouse finished his round and ran into the True Temper man.

"How were the clubs, Mr. Stackhouse?" he asked.

"I don't think they're for me," said Lefty, dropping a matched set of broken shafts at the man's feet and walking away.

CURTIS STRANGE

Two-time U.S. Open winner Curtis Strange is one of the game's really good guys. He's also one of its toughest competitors—one of the toughest that ever lived. Lee Trevino nicknamed him "The Piranha," because "if he gets a chance he'll eat you up." He's also candid and honest. For a time in the 1980s, he decided to skip the British Open. When Peter Andrews, an editor at *Golf Digest*, asked him why, he explained: "I like the British Open and I like playing over there. The problem is that every time I turn around some son of a bitch is telling me I have to play there, so I don't." Perfect.

Curtis's father, Tom, was a professional who worked for a time in Sam Snead's pro shop at The Greenbrier. He died from cancer when Curtis and his twin brother, Allan, were just fourteen. Anyone who was around the pressroom after Curtis won his first Open, in 1988 at The Country Club, saw a side of Curtis that until then had been seen only by his close friends and family.

"From the time I was nine, everything my father taught me about the golf swing is still with me," he said to a hushed crowd of writers, many of whom had known Curtis since his days as an amateur at Wake Forest University.

There was a pause as Curtis, drained from his 18-hole playoff with Nick Faldo, gathered his thoughts and tried to fight back his tears. He couldn't.

"This," he said softly, "is for my dad."

ALVIN CLARENCE "TITANIC" THOMPSON

Titanic Thompson pulled numerous hustles and scams over the years. One of his favorites was to arrive in a town and bet an unsuspecting schmo that he could toss an object—say, a grapefruit—over a tall building. After the money was laid down, Thompson would take the stairs to the top of an adjoining building and casually toss the object over the roof. Since he was known to carry a .45-caliber pistol, the bet was always paid off.

JIM THORPE

Jim Thorpe is one of the game's true characters. The son of a greens keeper, he grew up next to a golf course in North Carolina and learned the game playing money matches on public courses. His brother, Chuck, played the Tour for a while, but Jim was by far the more successful of the two, winning three Tour events. His swing is not exactly textbook material, and his view of the game is decidedly different from those of players who came up through the ranks of private clubs and prestigious amateur events.

Jim Thorpe left college, where he had earned a football scholarship, to concentrate on golf. To make ends meet, he worked for a few years in a General Motors plant near Baltimore. After a while, he figured that the only way to really improve his game was to get involved in some of the money games around town. One of the best players—and biggest gamblers—was a guy named Joe Pew, who favored bets of $500 a nine.

Thorpe knew that if he could beat Pew it would 1) prove to himself that he really did have a game good enough to make it on the PGA Tour; 2) establish him as a money player around town; and 3) help stake him to a shot at his tour card.

There was just one small problem: Joe Pew liked to see the money up front, and Jim Thorpe had exactly $104 to his name.

"I went to the bank and got a $50 bill and fifty-four ones," Thorpe explains. "I rolled the bills up, put the $50 on the outside, and wrapped an elastic band around them. Man, I looked like a Rockefeller. I got to the course and sort of flashed the roll to Joe, but told him I had to stash it because we were being watched.

"We went out and played, and when we got to 18 all I needed was a halve to win a grand," he continues. "The problem was that I only had one kind of shot, and that was a hook. I mean, I really had three kinds of shots: a hook, a big hook, and a hook that would go from here to there and keep running forever. This hole had trees all down the right side. There wasn't enough room for me to start the ball off the tee. My drive hit into those trees and came shootin' back at me. I thought to myself, 'Goodbye, money,' especially after Joe hit himself a good drive.

"I sort of knocked it up there towards the green and then Joe hits it three feet from the hole," Thorpe goes on. "I got up and skulled a pitching wedge. It was goin' about a hundred miles an hour when it hit the flag. The ball dropped straight down into the hole for a three. Man, I took that money, said 'Thank you very much,' and got out of there as fast as I could."

After fine-tuning his game with his own money on the line, Thorpe decided to try his luck on the Tour. But first there was the matter of raising the money he needed to give himself a real shot. Luck—and a certain amount of skill—took care of that.

He was playing in a local pro-am that was offering a car to anyone who made a hole-in-one. He made one, learned the car was worth $8,000, and sold it on the spot. After paying some bills, he headed for the qualifying school.

When he made it to the Tour, Thorpe became a particular favorite of Lee Trevino, who was generous with advice. The first time he was in contention to win a tournament, Trevino approached him on the putting green prior to the last round.

"Just remember, the other guys are just as nervous as you are," Trevino told him.

"Oh yeah?" said Thorpe. "Then there's goin' to be three guys throwing up on the first tee in a couple minutes."

Jim Thorpe came to the first tee in the opening round of the 1984 U.S. Open at Winged Foot. With the majestic stone clubhouse in the background and the gallery ringing the tee, the starter introduced the players and then added, "Gentlemen, play away, please."

Thorpe teed up his ball, took a look down the narrow, rough-lined fairway, and laid into the ball with his short, quick, powerful swing. The ball rocketed off the clubface and headed toward trouble—the rough or maybe even worse.

"Grow teeth, mother!" Thorpe pleaded in decidedly un-USGA fashion.

"I was in the locker room after one of my rounds in the 1978 PGA at Oakmont," remembers Thorpe. "Arnold [Palmer] was there and he had had a good round. He saw on television that Nicklaus had finished at 8 over. It was just pouring rain outside and Arnold said, 'Watch, Jack is 8 over and it's raining. That means they'll wash the round out.'

"Just then Jack walked around the corner and gave Arnold that look.

" 'Yeah, Arnold,' Jack said, 'just like they used to do for you.'

"Arnold turned bright red and they just kind of glared at each other for a second," said Thorpe. "I turned to the guys near me and said, 'Lord, let's get out of here. God and Jesus Christ are about to go at it.' "

LEE TREVINO

About the time Lee Trevino came on the Senior Tour he hired Chuck Rubin, Tom Watson's agent and brother-in-law, to represent him. Chuck had never shown a great deal of interest in learning the game, but one day he told Trevino he'd like to come down to Florida for some lessons.

"Chuck, I get $40,000 a day for an outing," Trevino said with a laugh. "How many days' worth of lessons do you want?"

Lee Trevino didn't come out on tour until he was twenty-seven, but he had learned he could handle the competition a few years before when he was working in the shop at the Horizon Country Club in El Paso, Texas. A group of members arranged for Raymond Floyd, twenty-two, to come down and play against a young unknown. Floyd, who was the Tour's Rookie of the Year, was used to playing money games and was looking forward to a $3,000 match against a player he'd never even heard of.

When Floyd arrived at the club, Trevino took Floyd's bag from his car, shined up his shoes, and asked if there was anything he could do for him.

"Just tell me who I'm playing," said Floyd.

"Me," said Trevino.

Floyd took one look at Trevino and decided he didn't even need to see the course.

They went out that afternoon and Floyd shot a 67. Trevino cut him by a shot. Floyd suggested they play another 9. Trevino said he had to go park carts, shine shoes, and clean clubs. Floyd just shook his head and went off to shoot doves.

The next day they went at it again, and again Trevino won, this time 66-65. Again, Floyd suggested they play another 9, and again Trevino said he had to go park carts.

On the third day, Floyd came out and shot a 31 on the front. The match came down to the final hole, and Floyd won by a shot. Somebody asked Floyd if he wanted to play again the next day.

"No, thank you," he said. "I can find much easier ways to make money."

L ee Trevino is a good friend of former president George Bush. One night Trevino and his wife, Claudia, were invited to dinner at the White House. Following dinner, they were all out walking one of the Bushes' dogs around the White House lawn. They approached a group of tourists standing outside that tall iron fence that surrounds the White House, and President Bush introduced Trevino to them.

"You don't have to tell us who he is, Mr. President," said one. "In Australia, he's more famous than you are."

HARRY VARDON

Harry Vardon, the winner of six British Opens and a U.S. Open, did much to popularize the game by conducting a series of exhibitions in the United States. One of his favorite trick shots was to place a ball in a shrub and then, taking an iron without much loft, send it rocketing straight into the air and have it land in the same shrub. And he would do it time after time, just to prove it wasn't a fluke.

KEN VENTURI

As an amateur, Ken Venturi was lucky enough to have his game shaped by Byron Nelson. When he turned pro—after almost winning the Masters as an amateur in 1956—he polished his game with advice from Ben Hogan, who saw in Venturi a person very much like himself: a perfectionist who was willing to dig the mysteries of the swing and the game "out of the dirt."

"In 1956, I came to the Masters for the first time," Venturi remembers. "In those days there was no special locker room for the Masters champions. Everyone shared the same room. We were having lunch and guys were making games for the afternoon. Sam asked Ben if he wanted to play. Sam said he would and asked Ben who he wanted as a partner.

" 'I'll take Ken,' Hogan said, 'and play anyone in the world.' "

Ten years later, Venturi's and Hogan's lives had changed dramatically. Hogan's magnificent career was past its prime, his last hurrah having come in 1960 at the U.S. Open. It wasn't that Hogan's singular shotmaking had failed him, but putting had increasingly become not only problematic, but even torturous. Venturi, whose career had produced fourteen victories, including a win in the 1964 U.S. Open, was struggling from the effects of carpal tunnel syndrome, a disease that cuts off blood flow to the hands.

"In 1966, the Open came to the Olympic Club in San Francisco, my hometown," Venturi says. "I was paired with Ben, and when we got to the second hole, a good par 4, Ben put it in there about twelve feet to the right of the hole. He got over the putt and just froze. He couldn't take it back. Finally, he said to me, 'Ken, I can't take it back. I can't hit it.'

"I just looked at him, gave a little laugh, and said, 'Who cares, you've beaten everyone long enough.'

"I'd like to say he made the putt, but he came close. A couple holes later, we were walking down the fairway after we hit our tee shots and he said, 'Thanks.'

" 'For what?' I asked.

" 'You know what for,' he said."

As a youngster growing up in San Francisco, Ken Venturi idolized Byron Nelson. One day Nelson came to town to play an exhibition and Ken went out to watch. On one hole, Ken worked his way through the gallery and inside the ropes. As Nelson prepared to hit a shot, Ken raised his little camera to snap a picture.

"Son, you should get back outside those ropes," Nelson said kindly.

That night Ken raced home and excitedly told his mother the good news.

"Mom, Byron Nelson spoke to me!" he said.

"What did he say?" she asked.

"He told me to get back outside the ropes," Ken said.

"Ken, that's not speaking to you, that's telling you what to do," she said.

"Yeah, but he was saying it just to me," Ken answered.

⛳

After battling back from a series of injuries and other problems to win the 1964 U.S. Open, Ken Venturi won three other tournaments before complications from surgery to correct carpal tunnel syndrome led him off the Tour and into work as an analyst for CBS Sports.

When the extent of the damage to his hands became known, he confided to his father that he was "scared to death."

"Dad, what if I can't play golf again?" he asked.

"Son, it doesn't matter," his father replied. "Even if you never hit another ball, you were the best I ever saw."

⛳

Somebody once asked Ken Venturi what his most embarrassing moment on a golf course was. He didn't hesitate.

"I was reading a putt on the 7th green at Augusta one year and my pants split," he remembers. "I had to wear my rain pants for two holes until I could get back to the clubhouse. It wouldn't have been so bad, except it was one of those really hot and humid days. People looked at me like I was crazy."

When Ken Venturi was a student at San Jose State he was already well-known throughout California as one of the best players, pro or amateur, in the state. Still, he was taken aback by a phone call he received one day.

"I was called out of a class to take a phone call," he remembers. "I was afraid something had happened to one of my parents, but when I picked up the phone the voice on the other end said, 'Ken, this is Bing Crosby. I've got a problem and I hope you can help me out. I need you to come down to Pebble Beach and play in my tournament. Can you do that?'

"Naturally, I thought it was one of my friends trying to pull one over on me," Ken recalls. "Even after I was sure it was Bing and I was telling my friends, nobody believed me."

When Ken Venturi was a young man his confidence in his golf game bordered on cockiness. His father, a down-to-earth man of uncommon wisdom, didn't exactly approve of his son's attitude.

In 1950, Ken won the San Francisco City Championship—a hugely popular win over an impressive field. At home after the match, he was telling his parents how well he had played. If he wasn't bragging, it was the next-best thing. Finally, his father had heard enough.

"Son," he said. "When you're really good, other people will tell you. You won't have to tell them."

When his career went into a tragic slump in the early 1960s, Ken Venturi became despondent and talked of quitting the Tour. He was broke, discouraged, and ashamed of the way he was playing. Once the brightest of young stars, he was now humiliated almost every time he teed it up. After returning to San Francisco, he told his father he was going to quit the Tour.

"Ken, you know I'll support whatever you decide to do, but just remember one thing," the older Venturi said. "Quitting is the only thing it doesn't take any talent to do."

Ken decided to give it one more try. He went to work on his game like a man possessed. He drove himself to get back into shape, despite the pain from injuries sustained in a recent automobile accident. He practiced relentlessly. Finally, as the 1964 season approached, he began to see glimmers of hope. Improvements were slow, coming in tiny increments, but they were coming nevertheless, and his confidence was returning.

That summer he capped his comeback by winning the U.S. Open at Congressional—a win most people rank as the most inspirational in Open history.

One of Venturi's colleagues and friends is Jack Whitaker, who remembers a particularly memorable round the two men played at Winged Foot.

"We had finished a taping and decided to try and squeeze in a round," says Whitaker. "Kenny didn't have his clubs, but we borrowed a set from the pro shop and I gave him a beat-up old sweater I had tucked away in my locker.

"We went out and Kenny was 1 or 2 under through eight," Whitaker continues. "On 9 he hooked his drive into the left rough. I didn't think he had a shot, and I'm pretty sure our caddie didn't think he had one, either. After Kenny studied his options, he pulled out an 8-iron and hit the prettiest little shot you've ever seen. The ball shot out between two branches and then began hooking back towards the green. The ball wound up about fifteen feet from the hole.

"The caddie looked at the ball and then back at Kenny. Finally he asked, 'Are you a pro?' Kenny smiled sort of sheepishly and said he was. The caddie said, 'If you come back here tomorrow dressed like that, we can make a lot of money for ourselves.' "

When Ken Venturi won the U.S. Open at Congressional, he had a local caddie named William Ward. Given the slump that Ken had been in coming into the Open, it's safe to say that the caddies weren't exactly fighting over his bag. But Ward soon became a big booster, always trying to keep Venturi's confidence up, always cheering him on.

In the years that followed, whenever Ken came back to the Washington area to televise a tournament for CBS Sports, he would make it a point to go to Congressional and find William Ward and give him some money—never less than $200—in appreciation.

LANNY WADKINS

L anny Wadkins, the captain of America's 1995 Ryder Cup team, is one of the best competitors and most-skilled players the country has produced in the past twenty-five years.

Lanny won the 1970 U.S. Amateur and then turned pro, winning twenty-one tournaments in a career that has been marked by occasional injuries. He won the 1977 PGA Championship in a playoff over Gene Littler at Pebble Beach.

After the awards ceremony, the party began in earnest. It must have been one hell of a party, too, because when Lanny awoke the next morning he couldn't find his winner's check. After a brief search it turned up, crumpled into a ball and resting in the fireplace.

TOM WATSON

Tom Watson is one of the greatest competitors the game has ever known—and one of its finest sportsmen as well.

Among all the honors he's received over the years, the one that he treasures most highly is being named captain of the 1993 Ryder Cup team.

The Ryder Cup matches at The Belfry in England were extremely close, but something Watson said at the players' dinner on the evening before the final matches offers a revealing glimpse of his confidence, which has helped make Tom Watson the greatest champion of his generation.

"You guys are going to win because I'm lucky," said Watson.

And he is. And they did.

TOM WEISKOPF

Tom Weiskopf is one of the finest ball-strikers the game has ever seen. But like so many skilled shotmakers, his putting has seldom been a match for the rest of his game.

In 1994, in his second year on the Senior Tour, he got a lesson from Lee Trevino that gave him a tremendous shot of confidence. He went into the U.S. Senior Open at Pinehurst with a lot of optimism about his play on the greens—even though he had putted horribly the week before.

"I feel like I'm the best putter in the world," he told a friend. "All these years I thought putting was the hardest part of the game. I was wrong."

The next day Weiskopf walked off the practice green and was approached by a fan, an older man.

"How's your putting, Tom?" the man asked.

"Super," said Tom. "I feel like I'm the world's greatest putter."

"Are you the same Tom Weiskopf that I saw on TV last weekend?" the man asked.

One evening during the 1979 British Open at Royal Lytham and St. Anne's, Tom Weiskopf, Ed Sneed, and writer Dan Jenkins went to dinner at the Clifton Arms hotel. Weiskopf ordered an expensive bottle of wine, but upon tasting it, decided it wasn't quite right.

"Dieter, bring us some ice and some club soda," Weiskopf told the maître d'.

Dieter arrived a few minutes later with the ice and water, and Weiskopf blended them with the wine.

"Now that's a good glass of wine," he said, beaming.

THE WILD KINGDOM

Sam Snead, who spent his boyhood hunting and fishing in the Virginia mountains, has maintained his passion for outdoor sports ever since. One day he was explaining to a group of writers how he used to catch trout by hand.

"You'd have to be pretty quick," one writer said.

"Nope," said Sam. "All you have to do is think like a trout."

🏌

"One day I was playing golf down at Pine Tree in Florida," Sam recalls. "I looked off there in the trees and saw this little bobcat. I used to catch them by hand when I was a kid, so I decided to give it a try. You have to get them by the scruff of the neck, just like a house cat, or you'll get scratched up pretty good. Well, I got him and put him in the side pocket of my golf bag. When we got back to the clubhouse, one of the fellas started to take my bag off the cart. I asked him to get my sweater out of the bag. He opened the zipper a few inches and that cat set to screeching and growling and scratching. I never did see anyone move as fast as that old boy did."

⛳

In the 1980s, a real estate developer in Florida came up with a clever marketing approach. He lined up several players on the then-fledgling Senior Tour to help promote one of his developments. In return, the players would be given either houses or condominiums on the property.

One of the players involved was Sam Snead. Sam loved nothing better than to go out and play a few rounds with his retriever, "Meister," at his side. Meister is an exceptionally well-behaved dog, and Sam's playing partners always readily accepted him.

Apparently, however, not everyone living near Sam's new property was happy about having Meister out on the course, and Sam was told that the practice had to stop.

"Well, if Meister's not welcome neither am I," said Sam, who promptly sold his property and moved.

⛳

A young professional, Paul Burley, was playing in the 1986 Phalabowra Open on the Safari (or African) Tour. It was Burley's first tournament, and he was understandably nervous—although not as nervous as he was soon to become.

Standing over his ball on the 3rd tee in the first round, he was just drawing his club back from the ball when there was an enormous crashing sound from the thick woods nearby. Burley wheeled around, and right before his disbelieving eyes was a charging hippopotamus. As his playing partners and their caddies scrambled up trees, Burley set off at full speed for the safety of the clubhouse, with the hippo giving chase.

Mercifully, Burley made it to the clubhouse and the hippo went on its way back into the bush. Still, it took several hours—and probably as many nerve-settling drinks as well—before the shaken Burley could be persuaded to leave the building.

A player named Jim Stewart was getting ready to tee off in the first round of the Singapore Open. As he reached into his bag for a club, he heard a hissing noise. He emptied the bag and, to his horror, saw an enormous cobra fall out along with his clubs. Immediately he grabbed an iron and killed the snake. Tournament officials were understanding, and let him move back his starting time.

Playing in the Nigerian Open one year, Philip Walton found himself facing a tricky shot from underneath a thick tree branch that would restrict his swing. He took his stance, made a couple of practice swings, and punched the ball out. As soon as Walton hit the ball, his caddie pointed out that a large snake was resting on the branch.

"Are you mad?" Walton screamed. "That snake could have fallen on me. Why didn't you tell me the snake was there?"

"I wanted you to hit a good shot and not worry about the snake," said his caddie.

Gordon Brand, Jr., was playing in Nairobi and noticed several monkeys in a stand of trees close to a tee. He and his playing partners gathered some nuts from the ground and threw them toward the monkeys. The next day, when Brand's group came to the same hole, they were showered with nuts by the monkeys.

Tom Sieckman is an American who honed his game on the foreign tours. He eventually got used to the variety of foreign courses and playing conditions, but frequently some of the local customs would leave him at a loss for words.

"I was playing a tournament in Asia and the promoters arranged a party for us," says Sieckman. "When it was time to eat, they brought out a dish that I didn't recognize. In fact, I'd never seen anything quite like it. I asked the host what it was.

" 'Monkey brain,' he said."

Sieckman begged off.

BABE ZAHARIAS

It could be argued that Babe Zaharias was the finest woman athlete in American history. After a brilliant career in track and field, she turned to golf. Her greatest triumph was in 1954, when she came back from cancer surgery to win the U.S. Women's Open at Salem Country Club outside of Boston.

Zaharias was married to George Zaharias, a popular wrestler. He was dark-haired and handsome and something of a sex symbol among women wrestling fans, of which there were surprisingly many in those days. Still, Babe couldn't resist needling him.

"George, when we got married you were a Greek god," she said. "Now you're just a goddamn Greek."

When Babe won the 1947 British Women's Amateur Championship it made for huge headlines on both sides of the Atlantic. When she arrived in New York City aboard the *Queen Elizabeth* there was a huge crowd awaiting her arrival. She didn't disappoint them. She appeared at the head of the gangplank wearing a kilt, then did a respectable Highland Fling down the gangplank before diving into her husband's waiting arms.

When Babe and her husband returned to Denver, where they were living at the time, the city turned out for a huge celebration that featured the presentation of an enormous key to the city, which took several men to carry to the stage. As she watched the men labor with the key, she quipped, "Don't worry, fellas. You just get it up here. George will carry it home."

The Babe had a genius for creating publicity, not only for herself but for the women's tour in general. At a tournament in Chicago, she was paired with a very good amateur from the Midwest. They were eating breakfast prior to their round, and Babe tried to talk the girl into turning pro and joining the Tour.

"What do I have to do to actually become a pro?" the girl asked.

"It's simple," said Babe, putting her hand on the girl's head. "Raise your right hand and repeat after me: 'I am a pro.'"

The girl did as she was told.

"Well, that's it, kid," said Babe. "Now you just go out there to the first tee and tell them Babe said you're a pro."

The Babe was playing in a pro-am, and one of her partners was obviously unnerved by playing with Babe in front of a big gallery.

He got over the ball, made several nervous waggles, and accidentally knocked the ball off the tee. He apologized, reteed the ball, and began the process all over again. When he finally connected, the ball shot off to the right, squarely struck a tree, and headed back toward the tee, prompting Babe and the other players to scatter.

"Sir, let me give you a piece of advice I learned when I first took up this game," she said. "The first rule of golf is 'Always make sure the ball winds up in front of you after you hit it.' "

A writer once asked Babe what she did when men tried to hit on her.

"It depends on my mood and what the guy looks like," she quipped. "Sometimes I let him and sometimes I kick the hell out of him."

And she actually did just that one day in a clubhouse bar. She had played badly and was in no mood to be bothered. But the man was persistent, and the next thing he knew, he was spread-eagled on the floor. Babe went back to her bar stool and finished her drink in peace.

Babe Didriksen Zaharias was a celebrity of enormous proportion. Her death on September 27, 1956, was front-page news across the country. The following day, President Eisenhower began a news conference with a personal remembrance of Babe.

FUZZY ZOELLER

Fuzzy Zoeller is a marvel of sorts. Because he has a bad back caused by a high school basketball injury, he's forced to play a limited schedule—usually fewer than twenty tournaments a year. In spite of this, he has won ten times on tour, including two majors—the 1979 Masters and the 1984 U.S. Open. Strangely enough, he won both his majors in playoffs, beating Ed Sneed and Tom Watson at Augusta and Greg Norman at Winged Foot.

He won universal praise for his sportsmanship in the fourth round at Winged Foot in the '84 Open. Standing in the 18th fairway, he watched Greg Norman hole a long, difficult par putt on the final green. Thinking it was for a birdie and a likely win, Fuzzy took the white towel from his bag and waved it toward Norman in surrender. He then went on to tie Norman, forcing the playoff, which he won easily.

But for all his talent and victories, he's just as well known for his sense of humor, and this combination of attributes has helped make him one of the most popular players in pro-ams and clinics. Apparently, some of that wit has rubbed off on his caddie, Mike Mazzeo.

A writer was doing a story on caddies who had been with the same players for an unusually long time. Mike

Mazzeo has worked with Zoeller almost from the time he joined the Tour in 1975. In the course of the interview, the writer asked Mazzeo why he was able to keep his job for so long while other caddies bounced from bag to bag.

Was it because he was so good helping with club selection? No.

Was it because he was so reliable? No.

Was it because he was a calming influence under pressure? No.

Well, the writer asked, why was it that he was able to stay with Fuzzy for so long?

"I know too much," said Mazzeo. "He's afraid to fire me."

Fuzzy Zoeller is part of the answer to one of the best golf trivia questions of all time: Which player(s) won the Masters the first time he played in it?

The answer is Fuzzy Zoeller (1979), Gene Sarazen (1935), and Horton Smith (1934, the first year the tournament was played).

INDEX